I0467727

A Beginner's Guide To Drawing Creative Flower Tattoos

Easy Way To Draw Flower Tattoos

Flower Tattoos

By : Gala Publication

2

Published By :

Gala Publication
© Copyright 2015 – Gala Publication

ISBN-13: **978-1522707752**
ISBN-10: **1522707751**

Table of Contents

DAHLIA FLOWER TATTOO

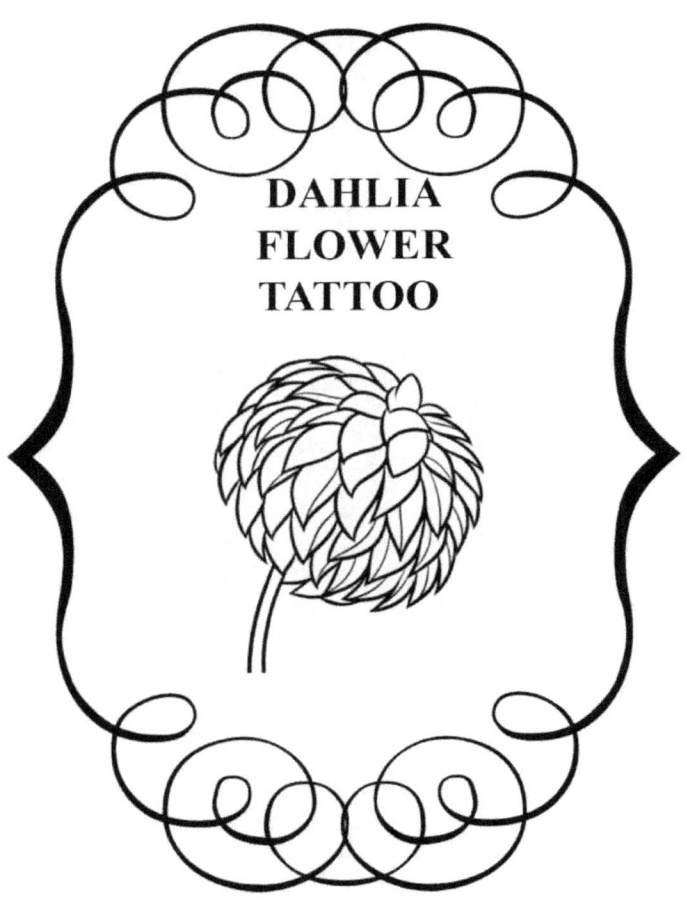

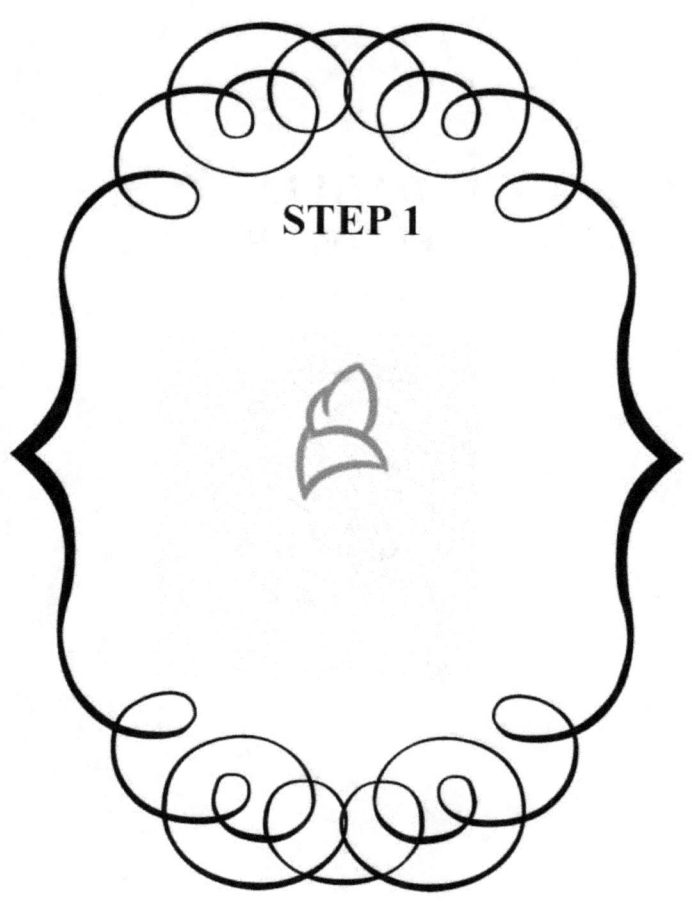

STEP 1

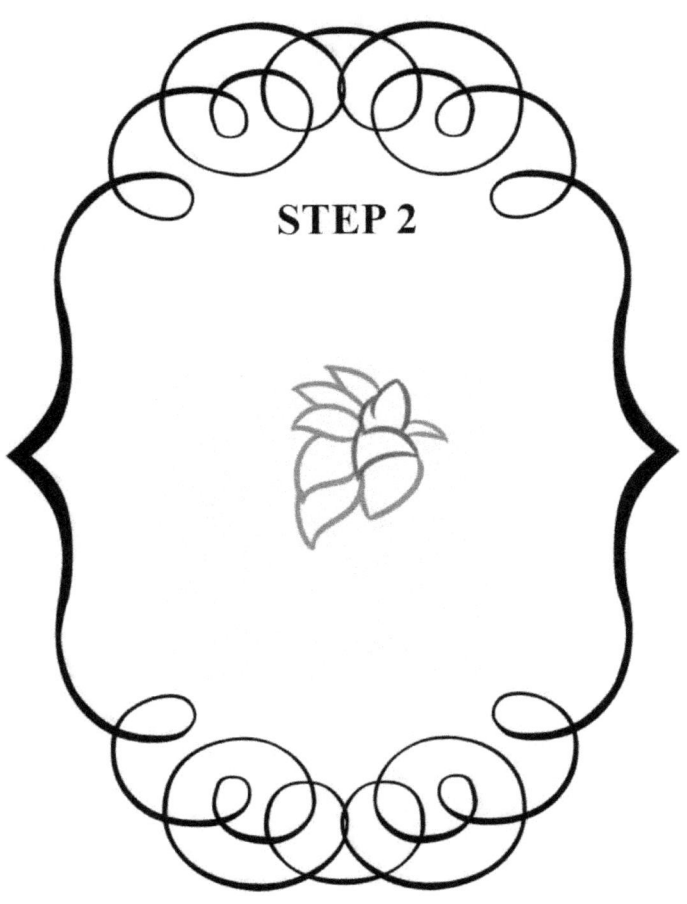

STEP 2

STEP 3

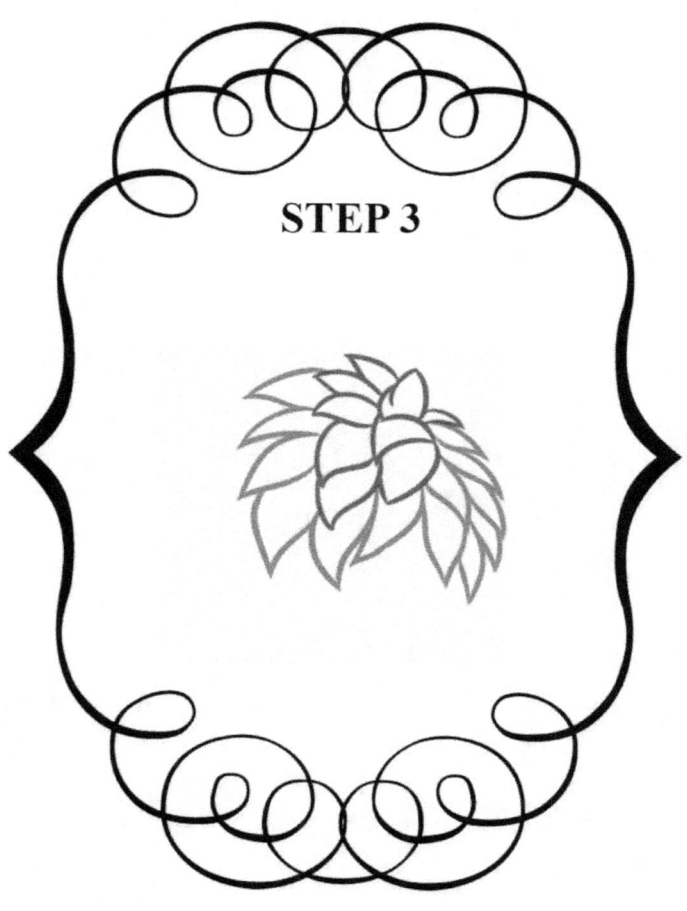

STEP 4

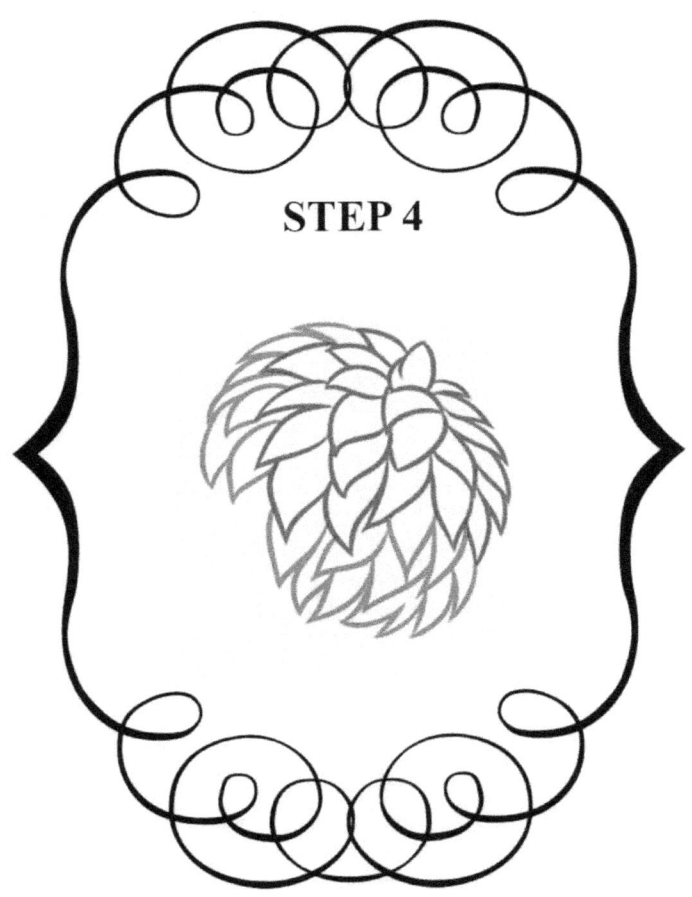

10

STEP 5

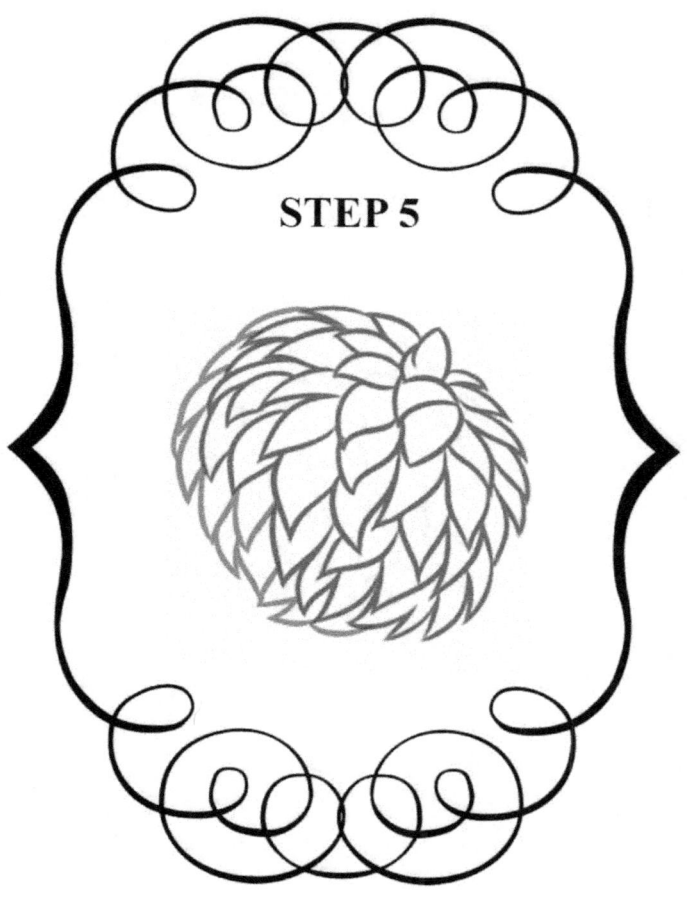

STEP 6

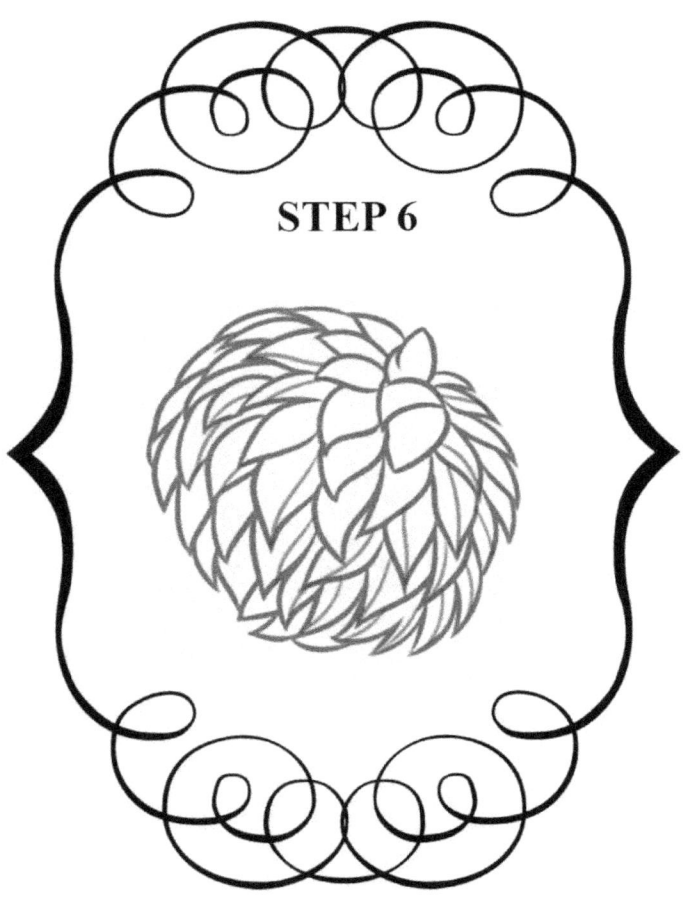

STEP 7

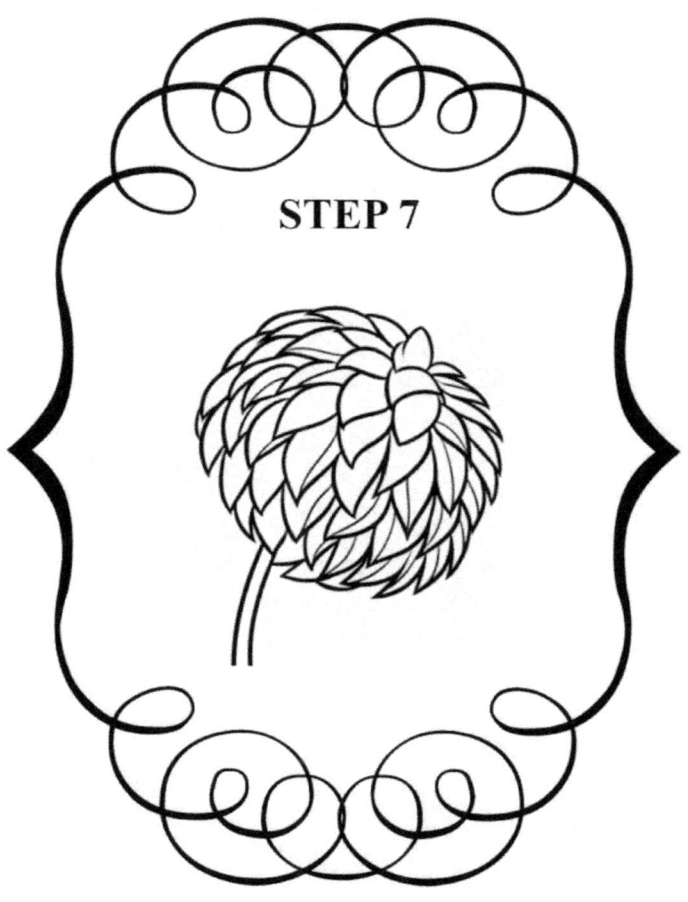

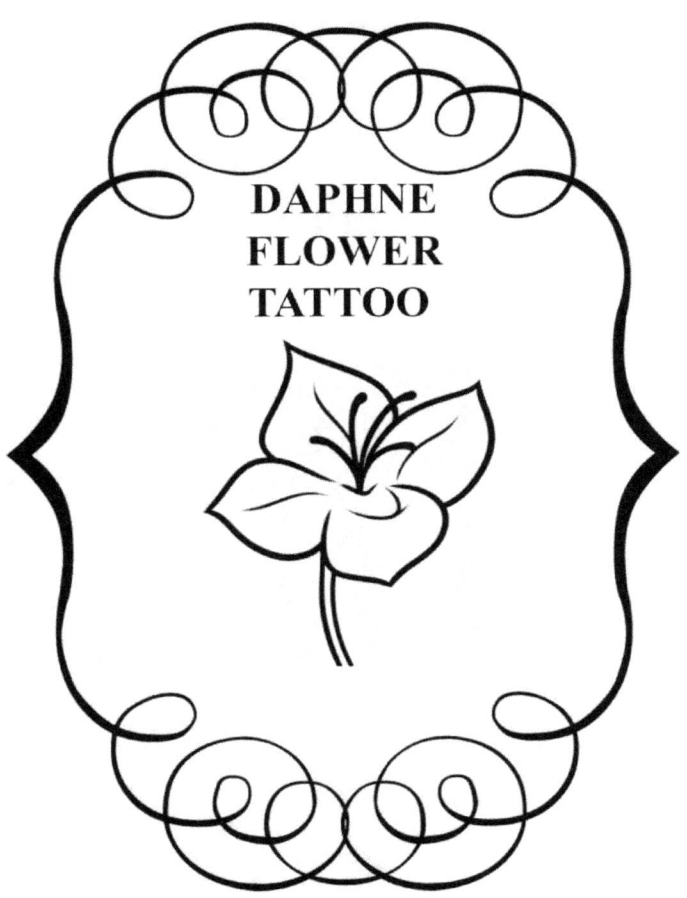

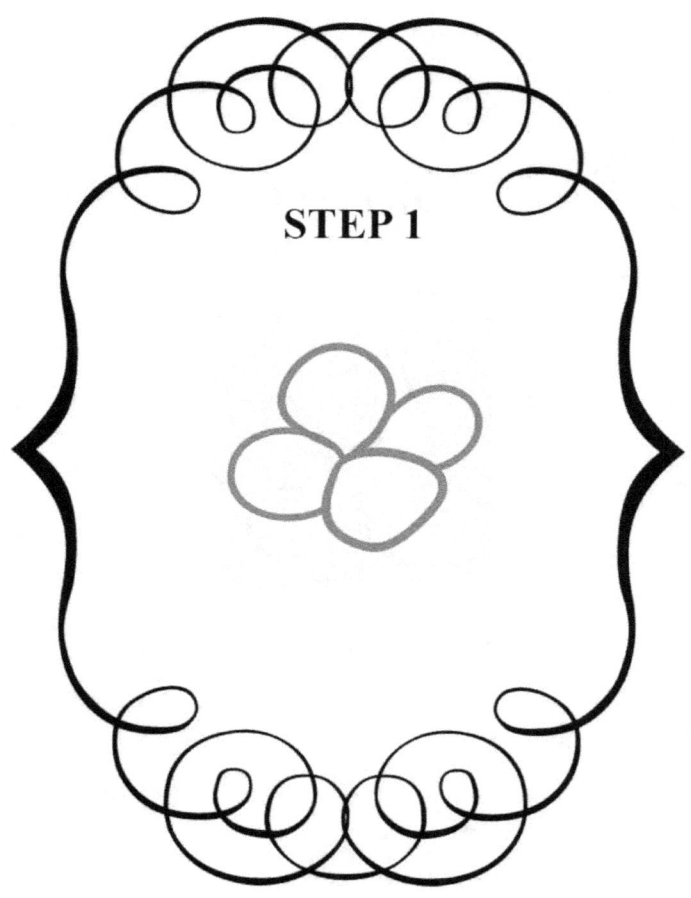

STEP 1

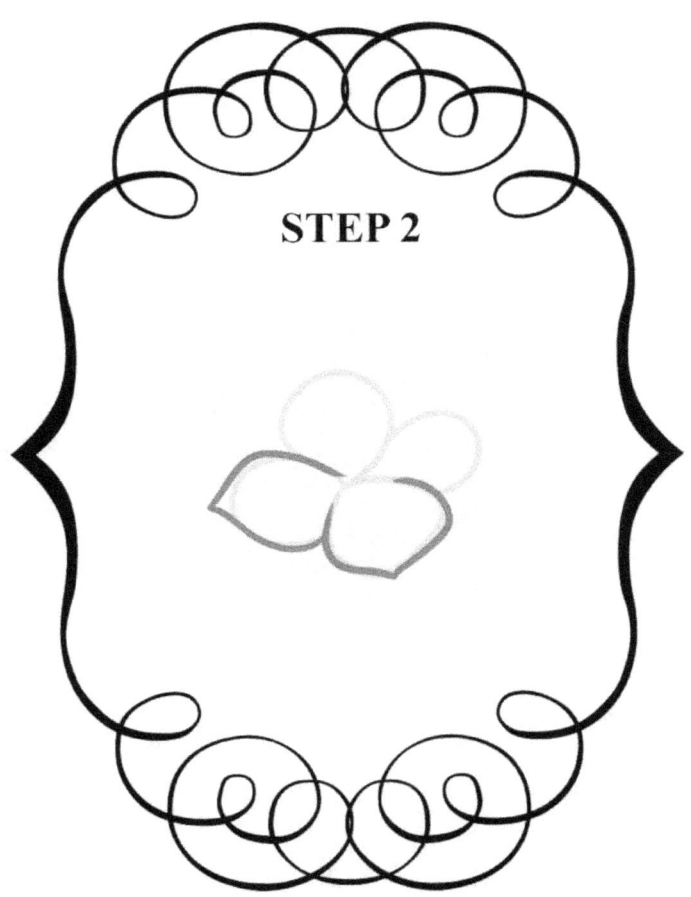

STEP 2

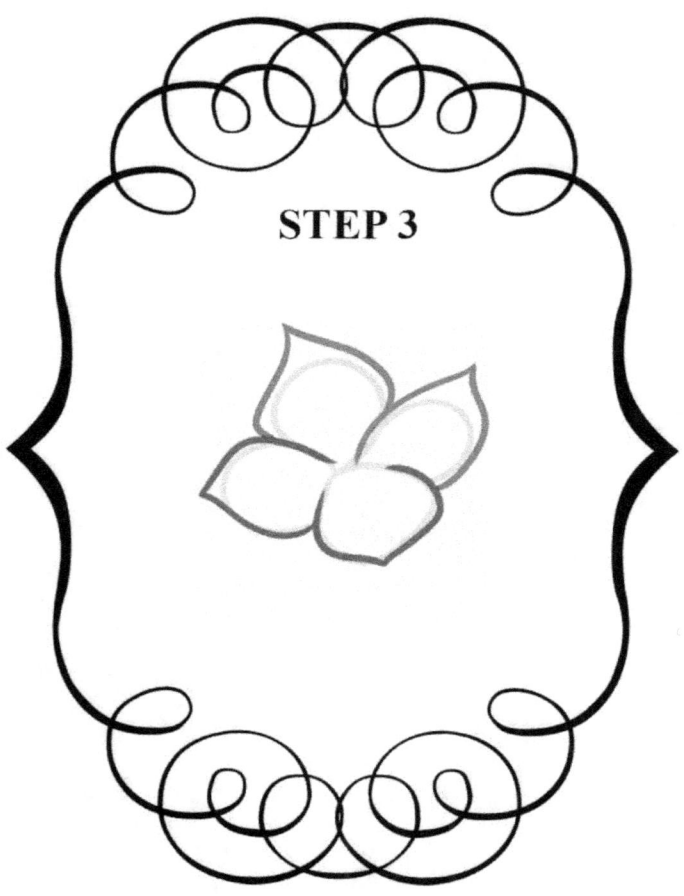

STEP 3

STEP 4

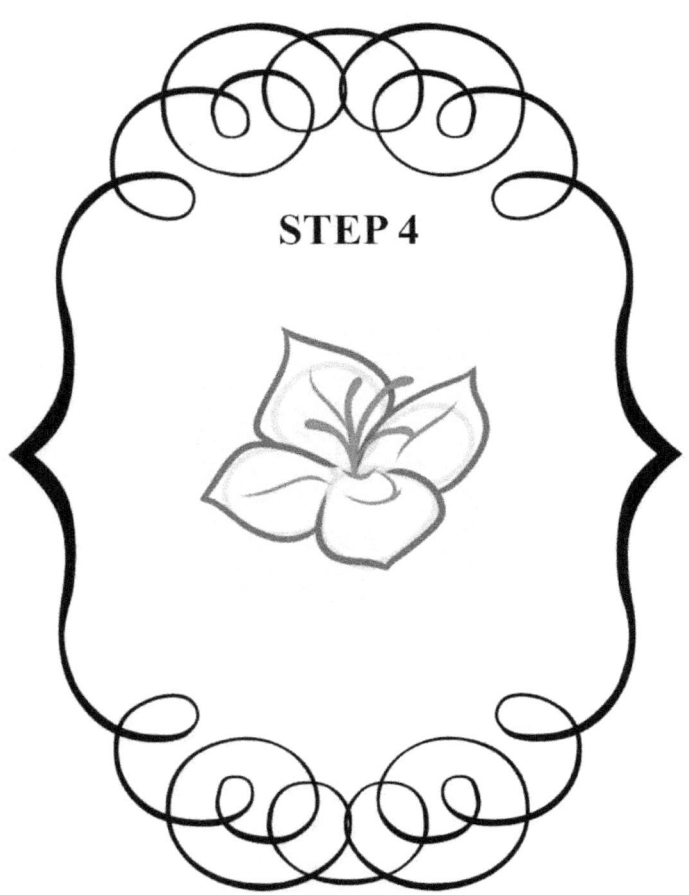

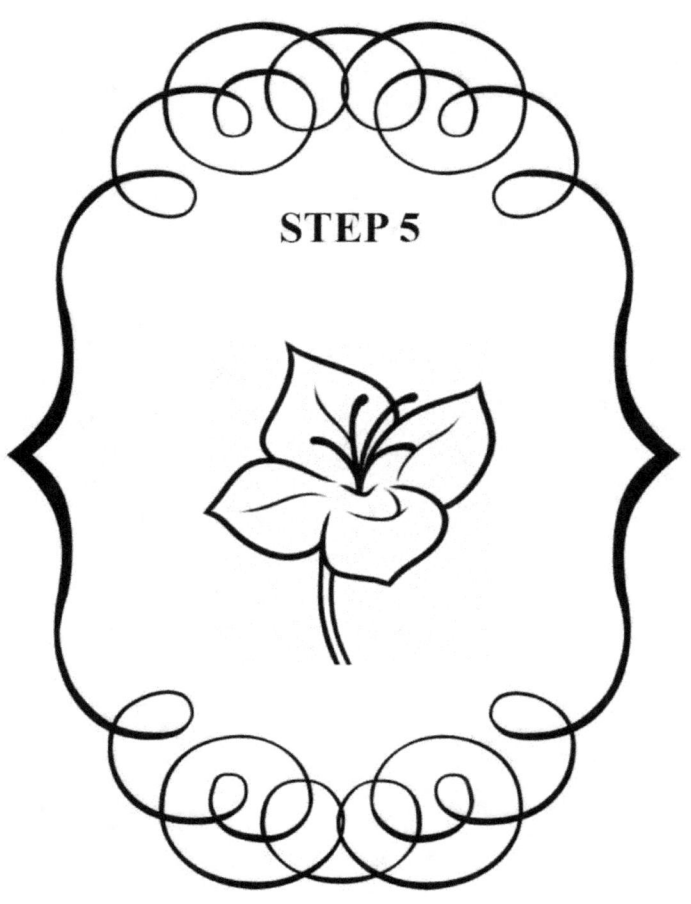

STEP 5

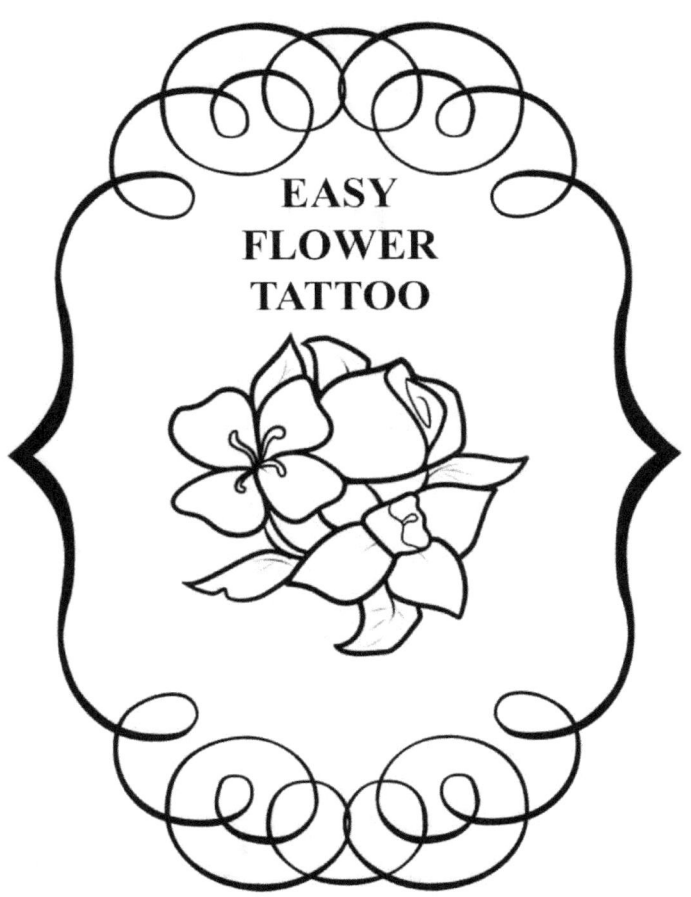

EASY
FLOWER
TATTOO

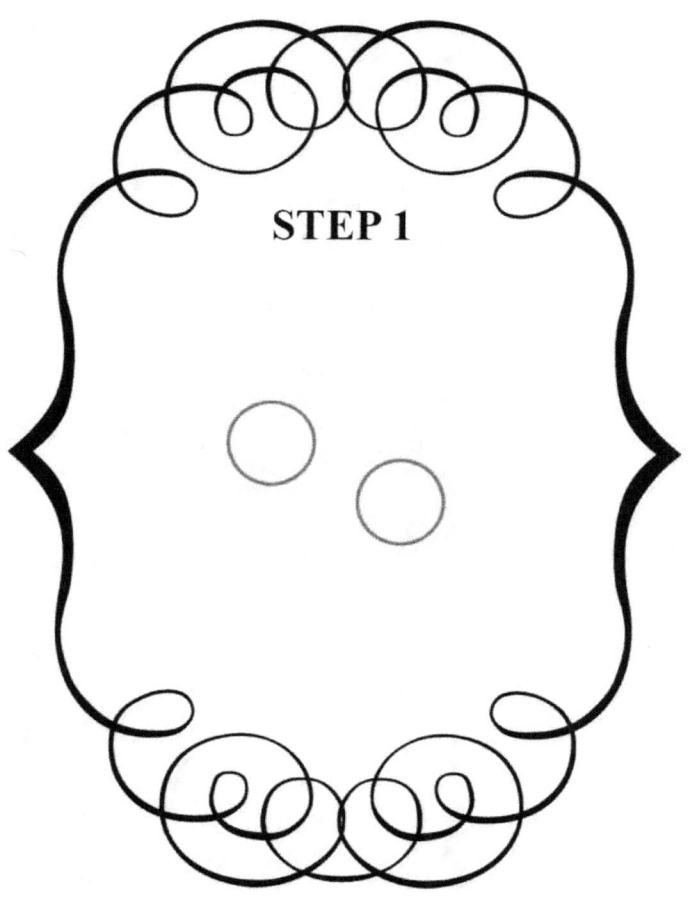

STEP 1

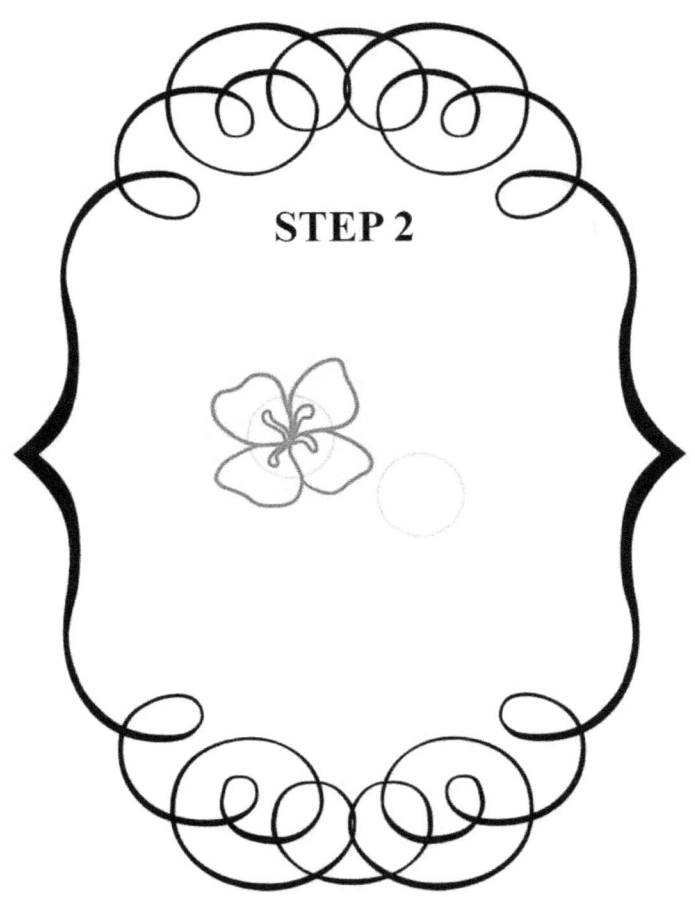

STEP 2

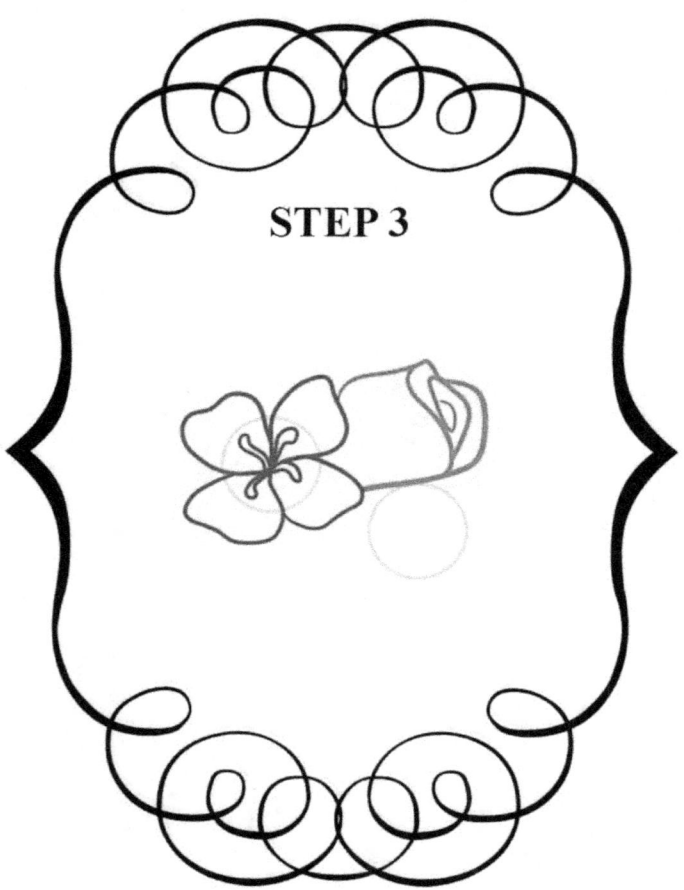

22

STEP 3

STEP 4

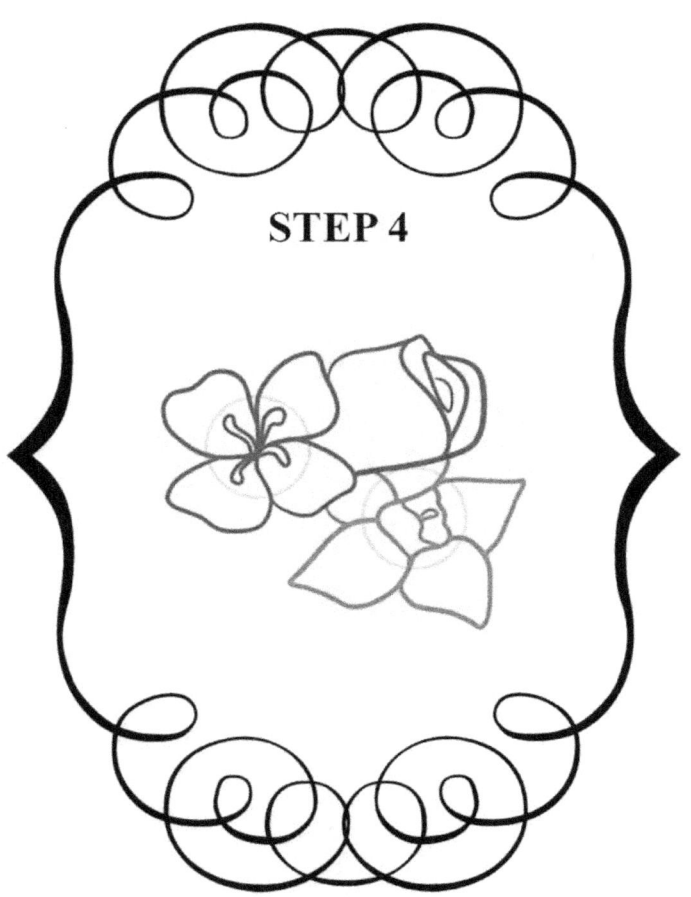

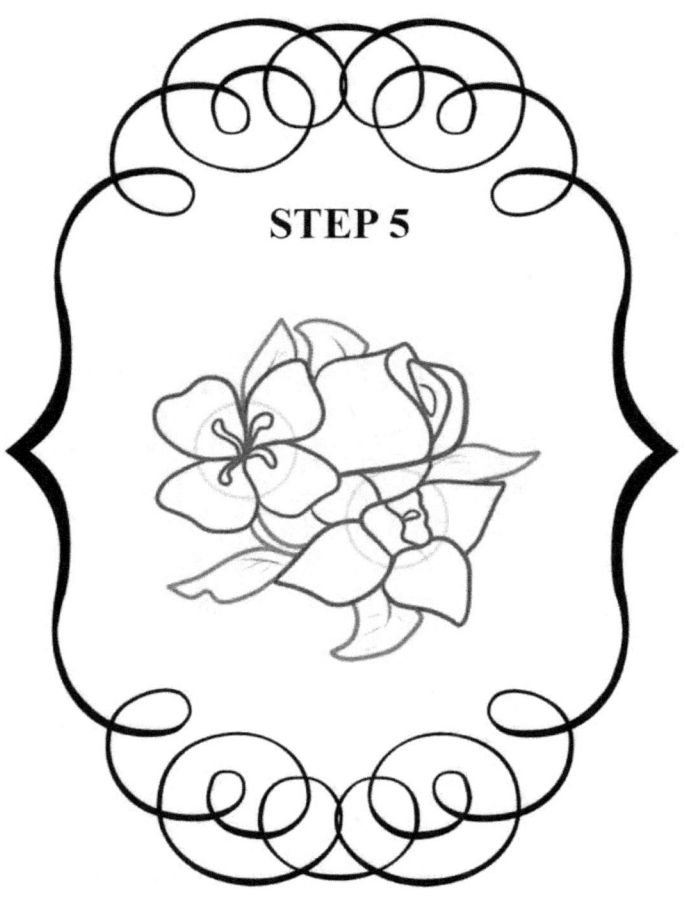

STEP 6

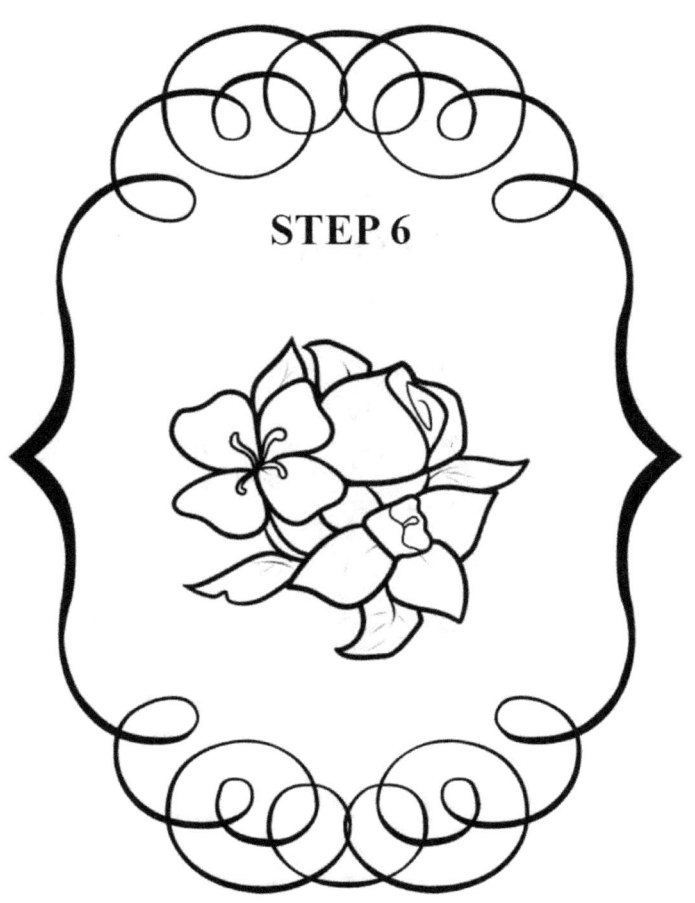

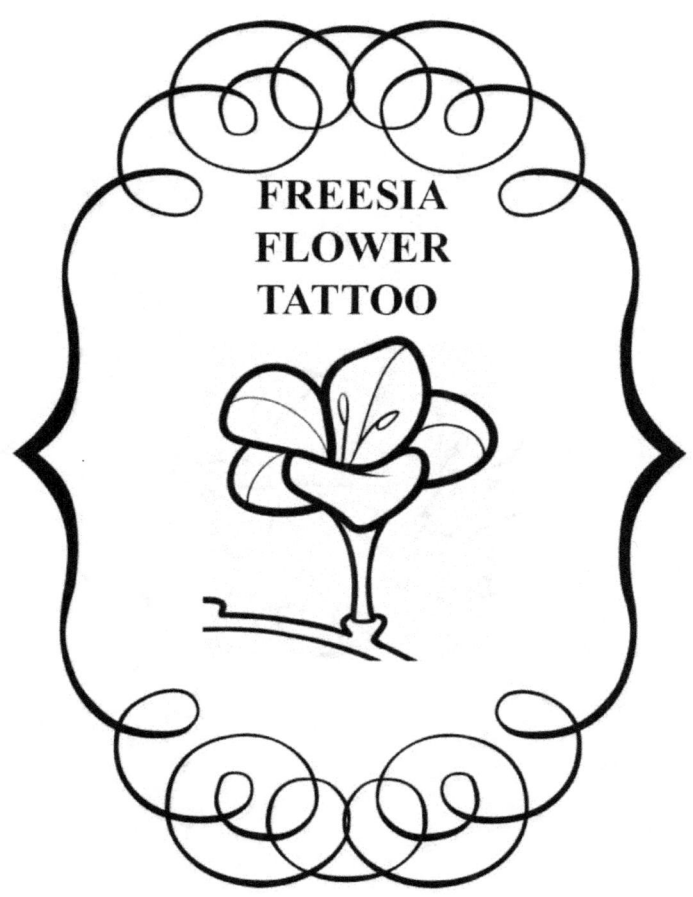

FREESIA
FLOWER
TATTOO

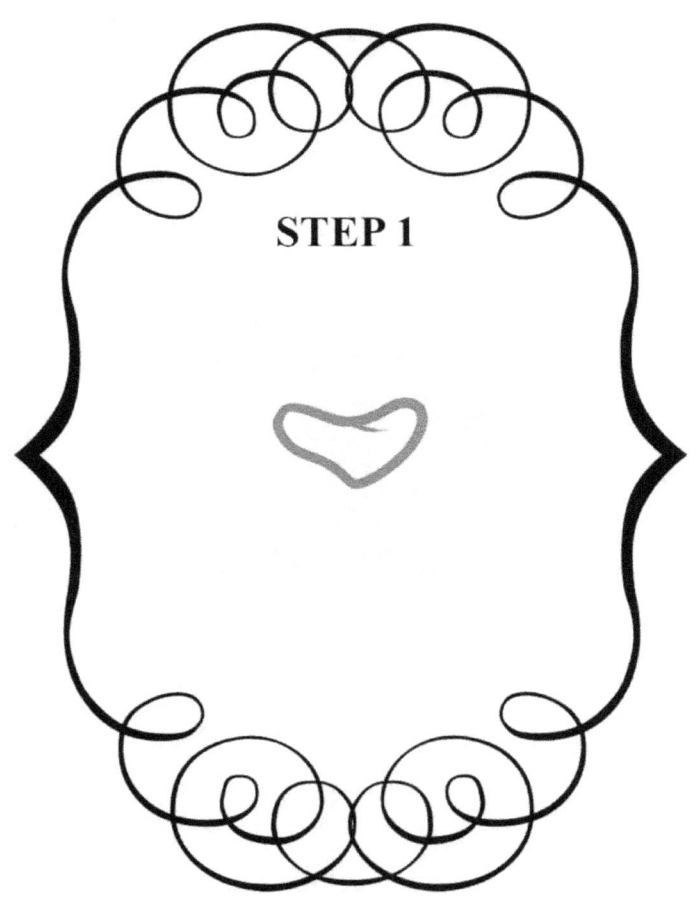

STEP 1

STEP 2

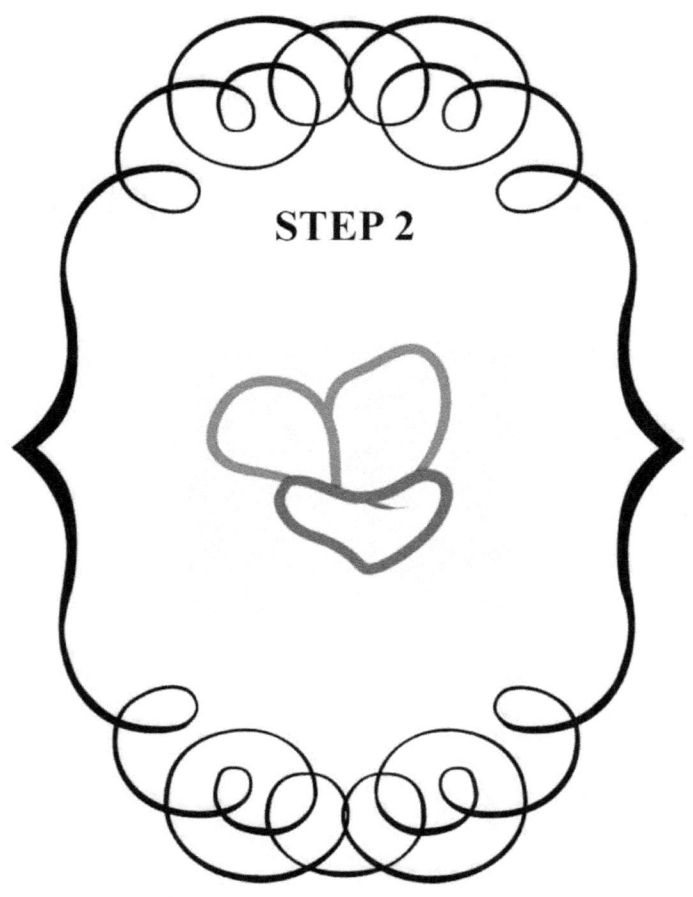

STEP 3

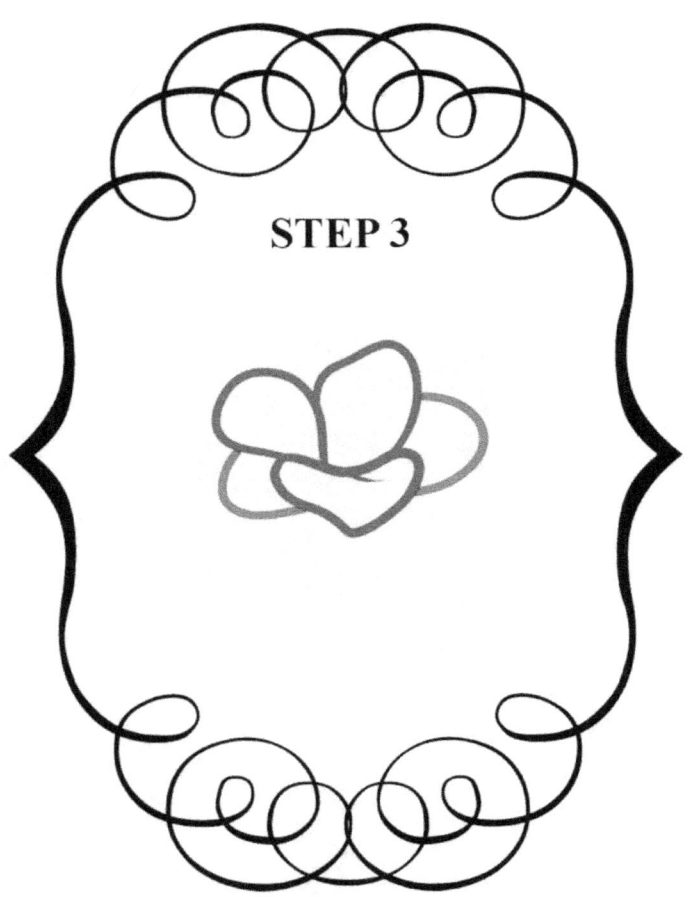

30

STEP 4

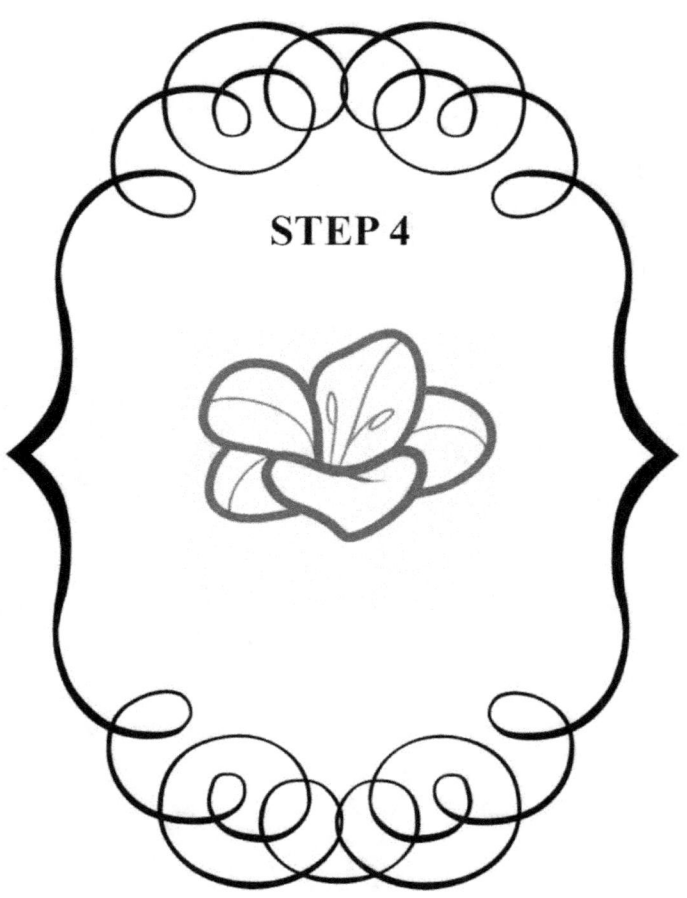

STEP 5

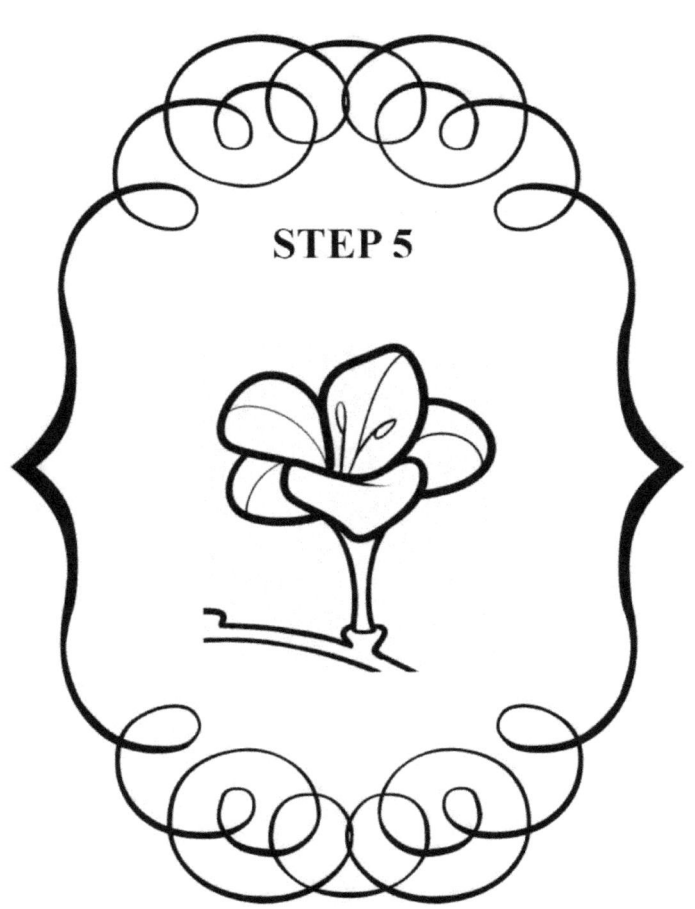

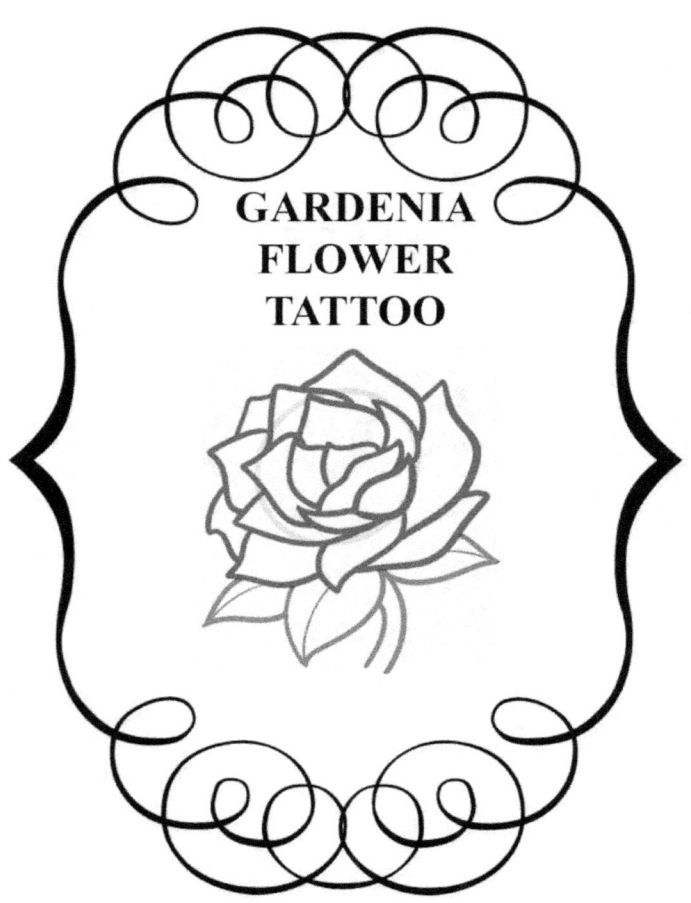

GARDENIA
FLOWER
TATTOO

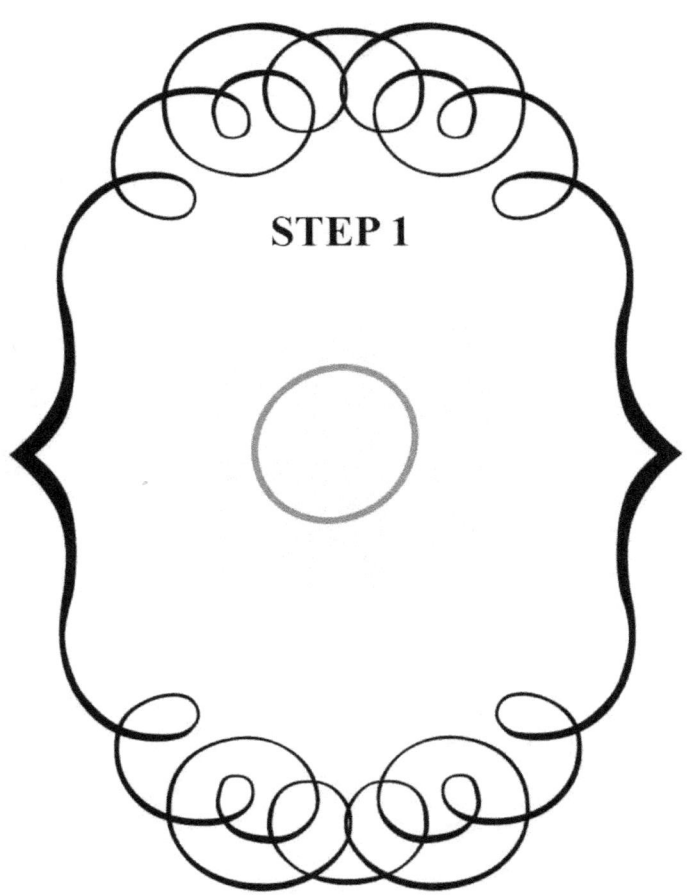

STEP 1

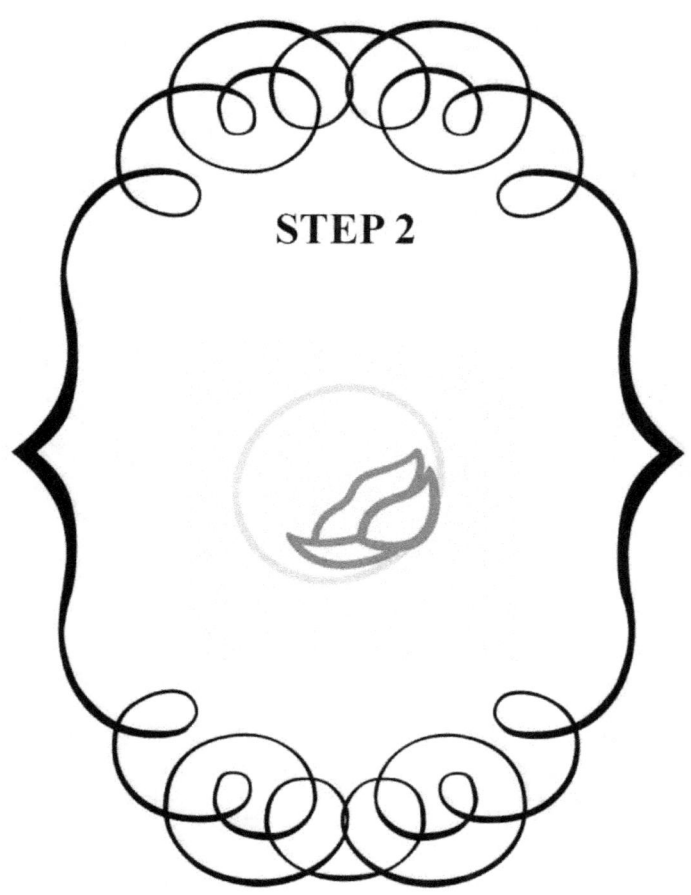

STEP 2

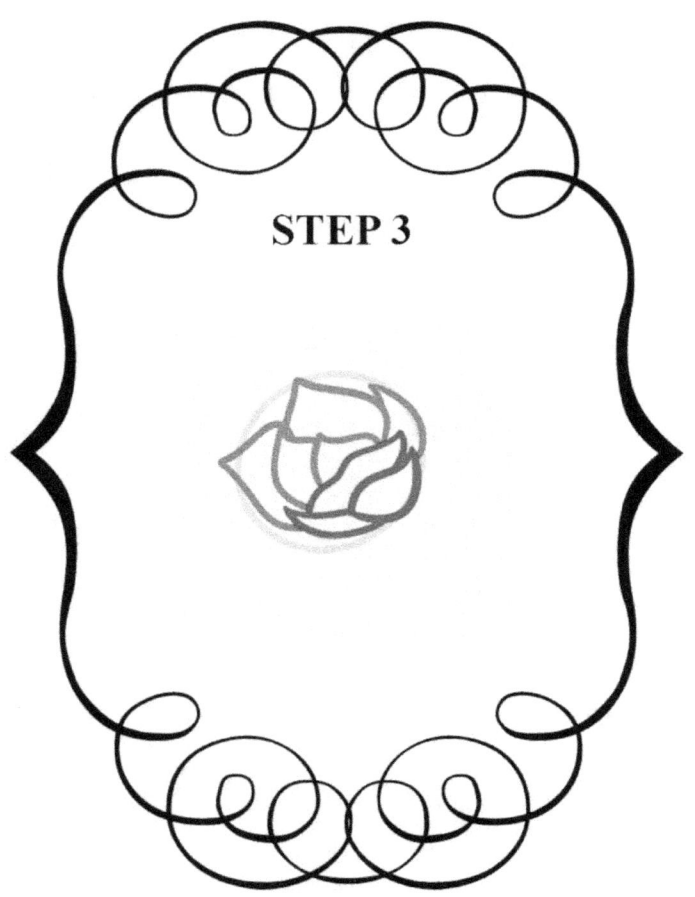

STEP 3

STEP 4

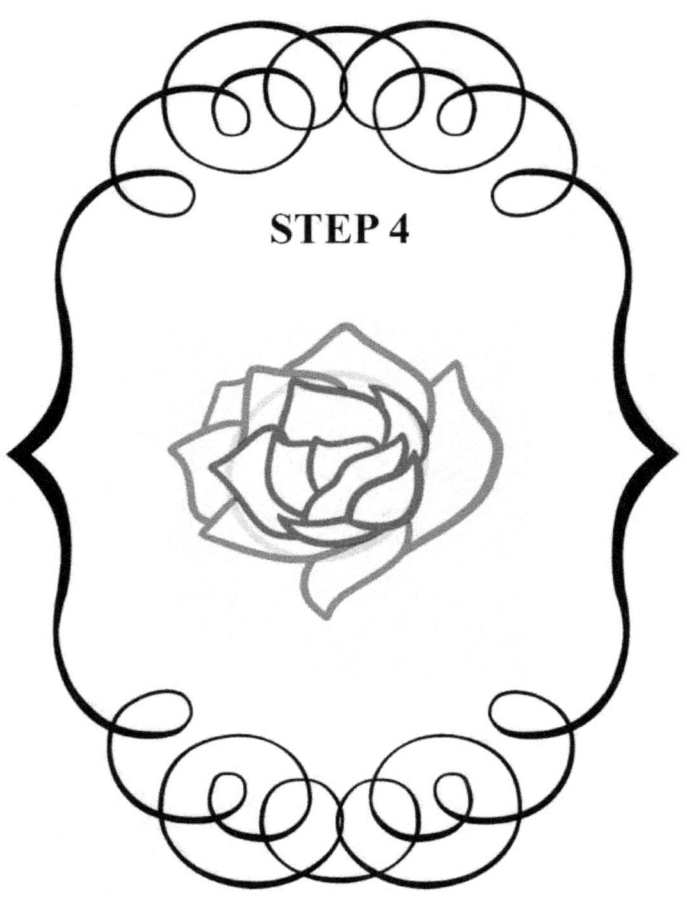

STEP 5

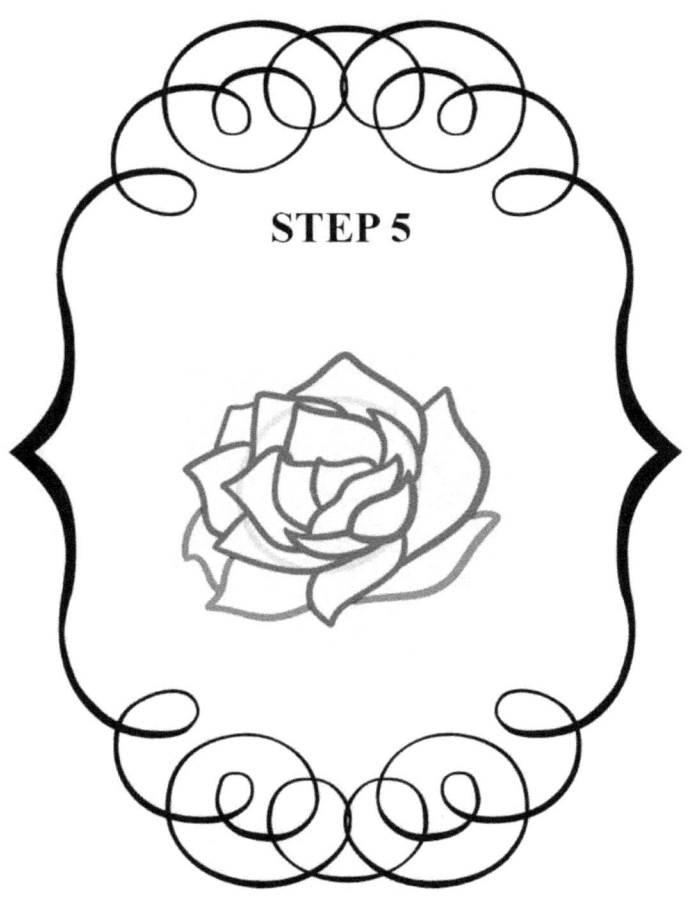

STEP 6

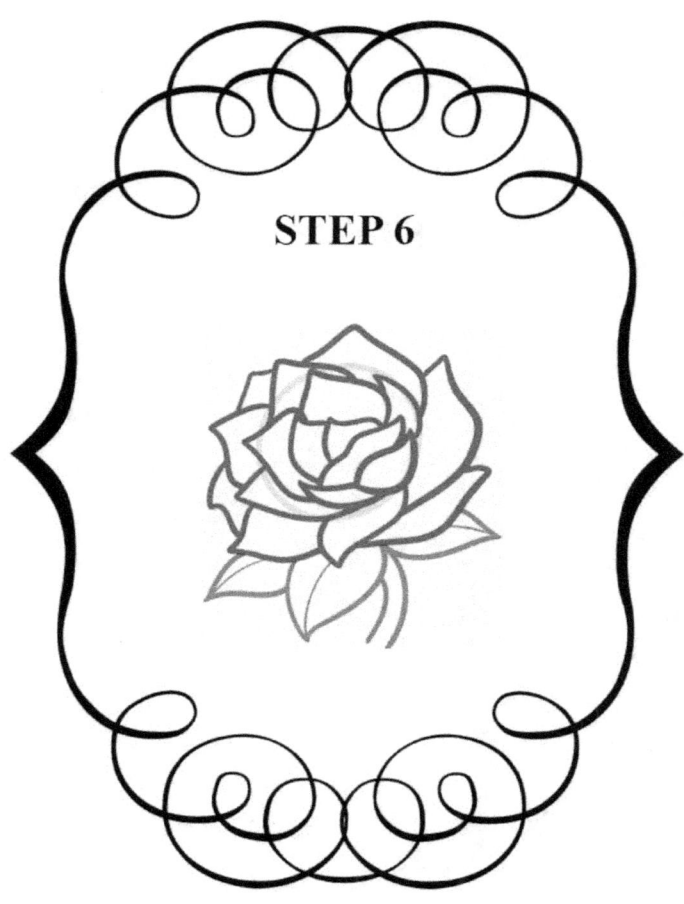

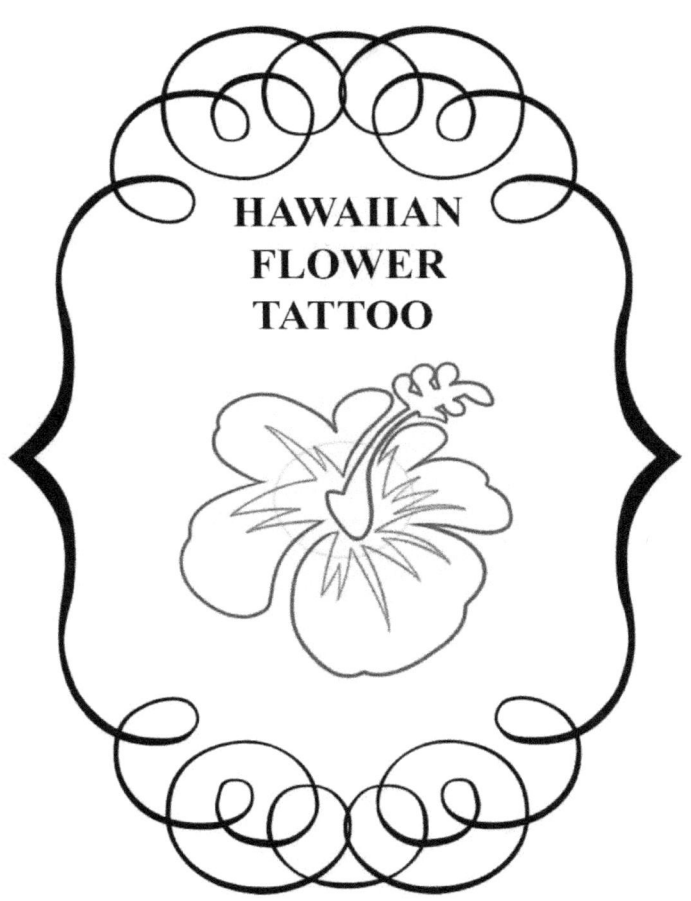

HAWAIIAN
FLOWER
TATTOO

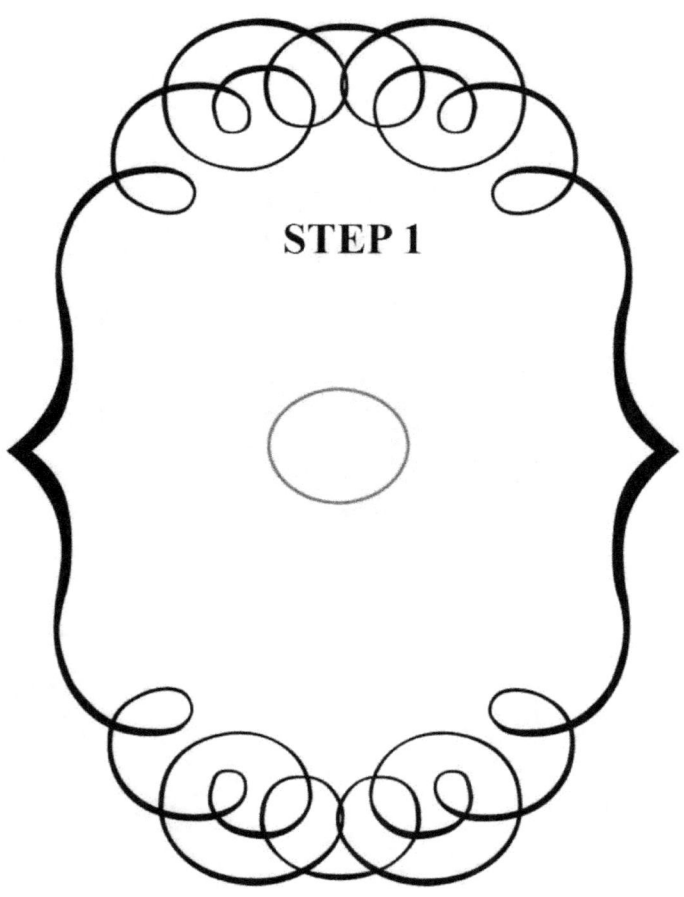

STEP 1

STEP 2

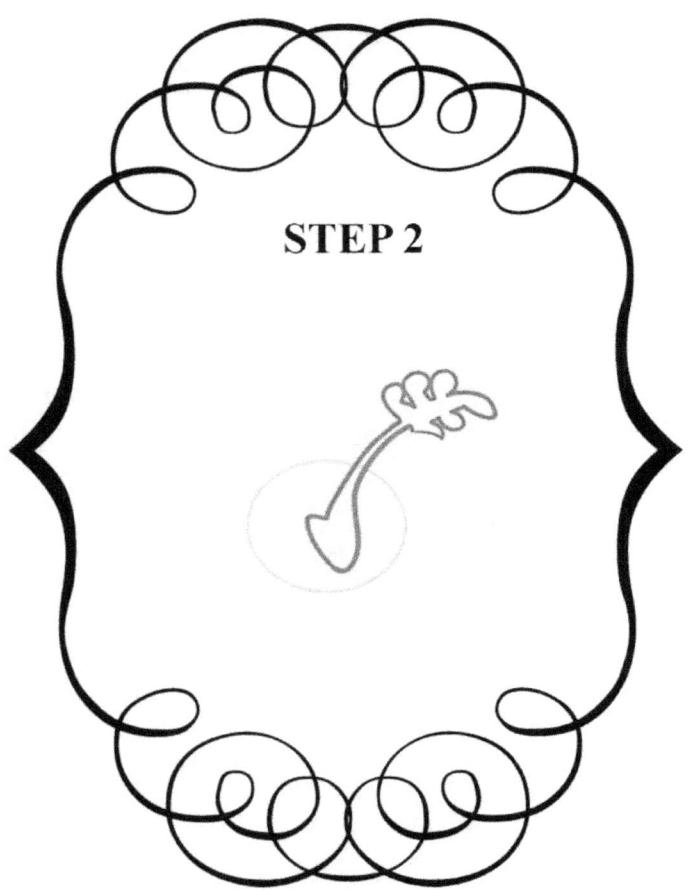

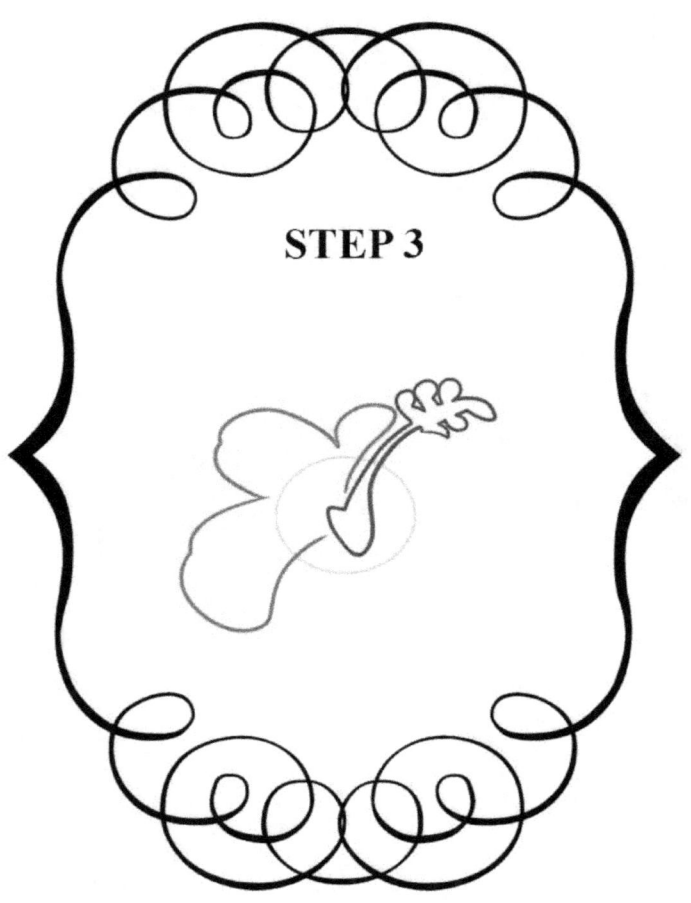

STEP 3

STEP 4

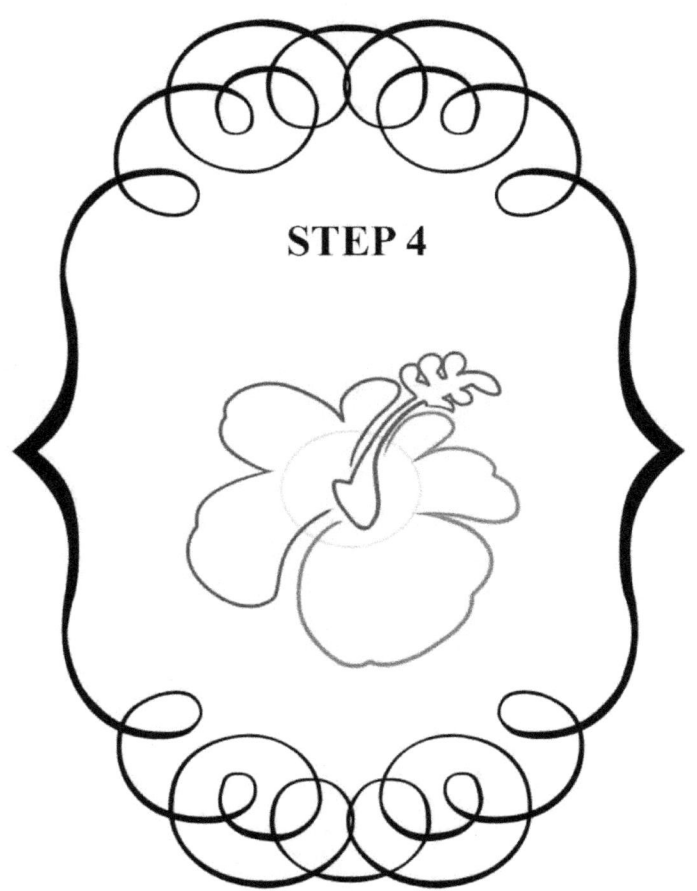

STEP 5

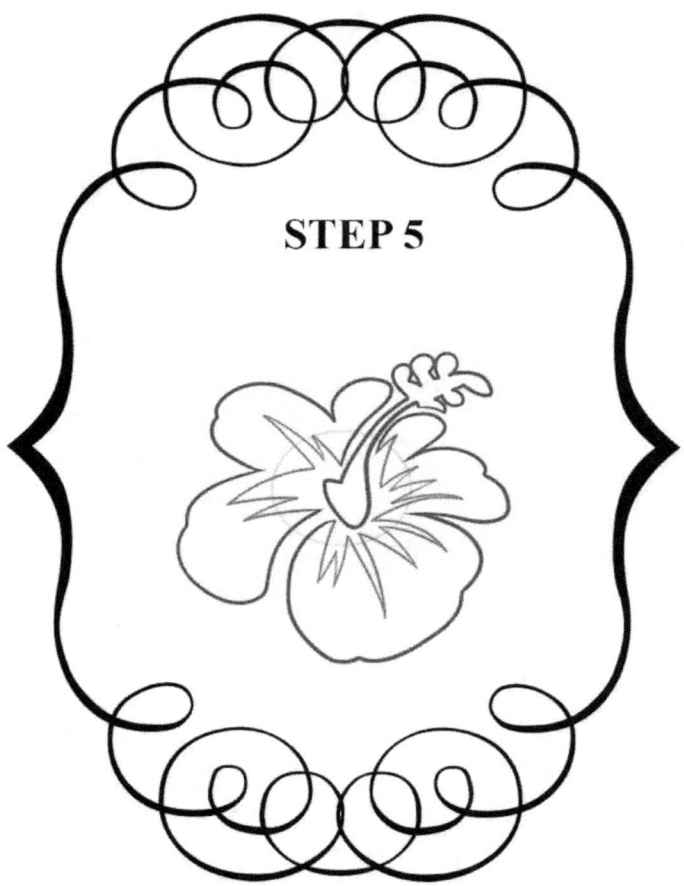

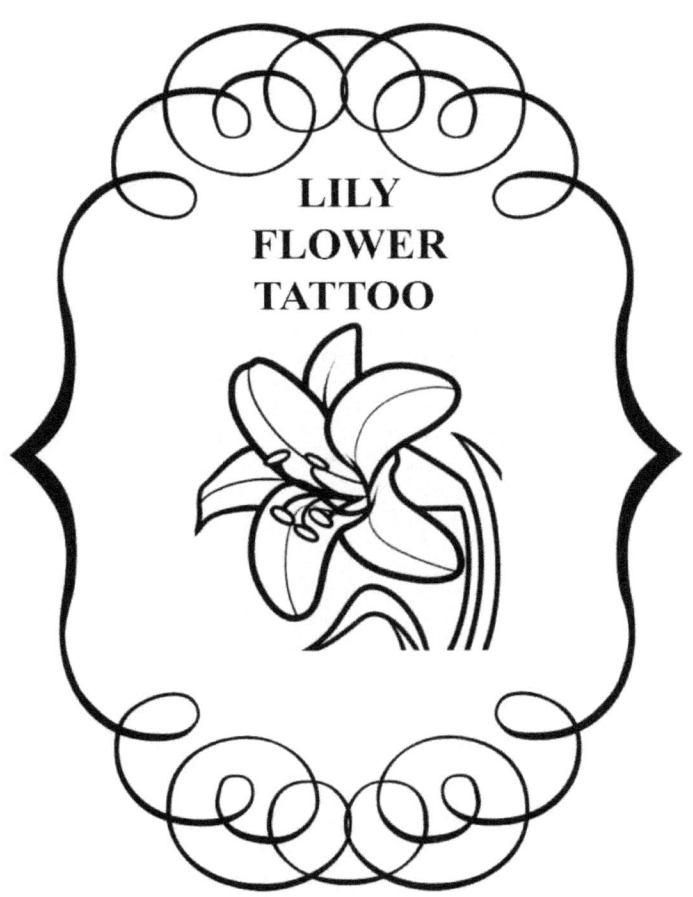

LILY
FLOWER
TATTOO

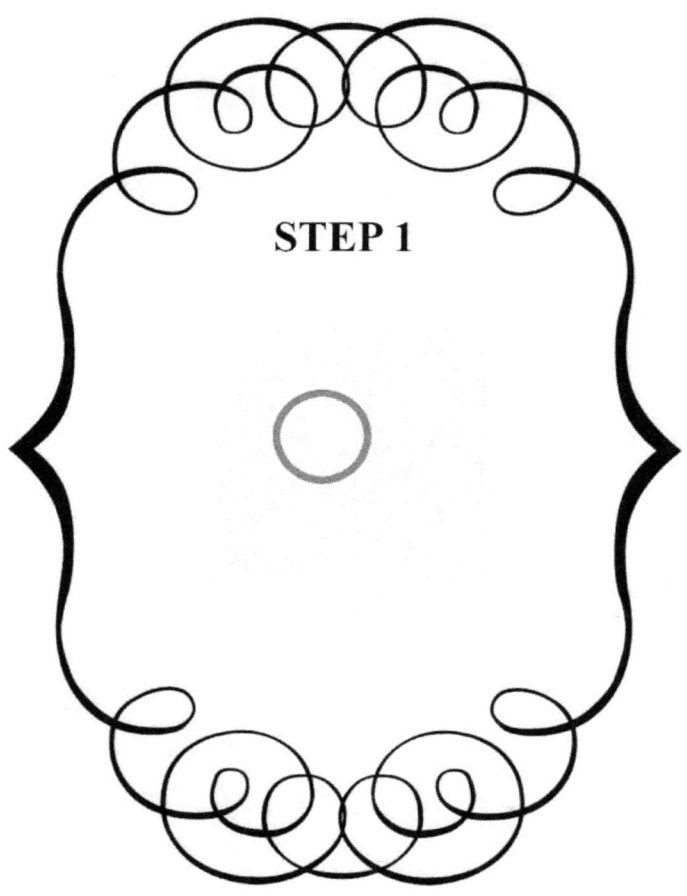

STEP 1

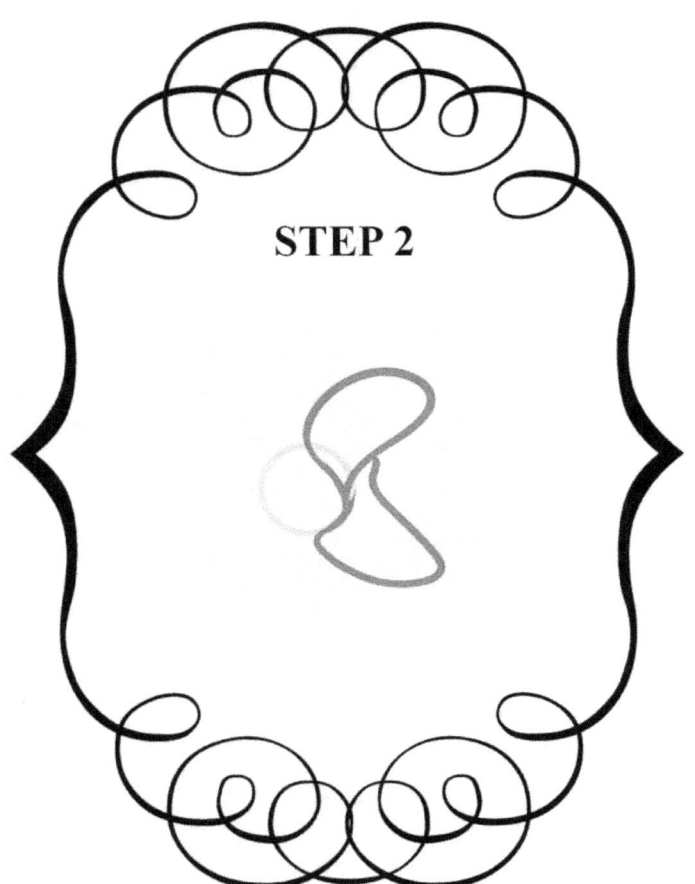

STEP 2

48

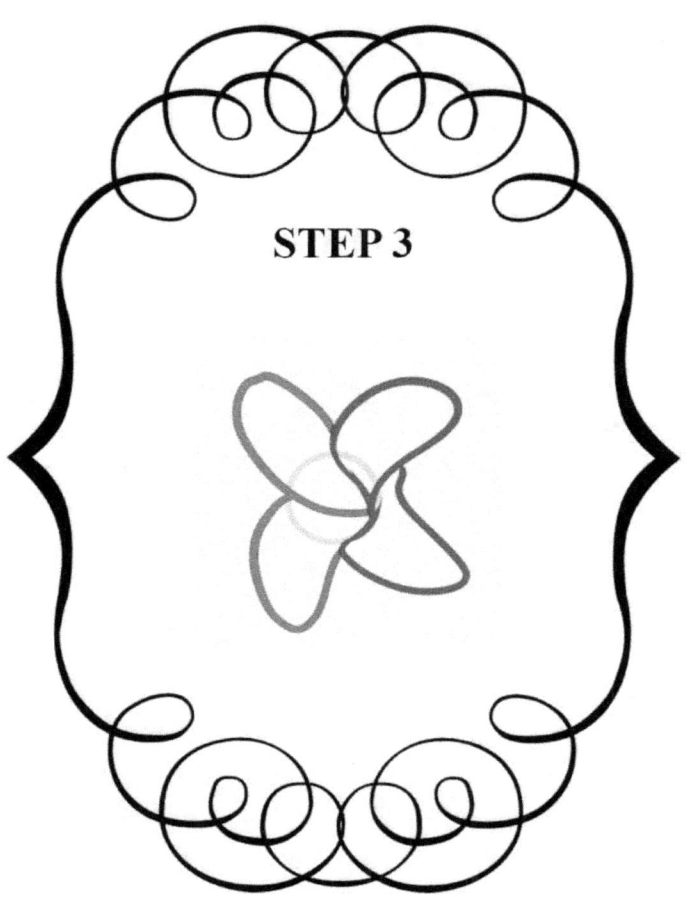

STEP 3

STEP 4

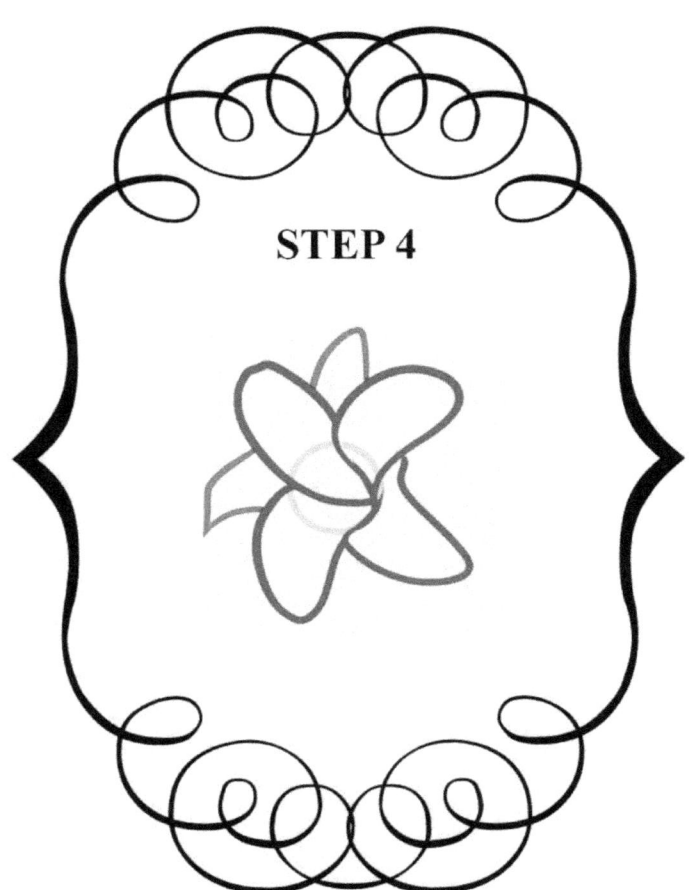

STEP 5

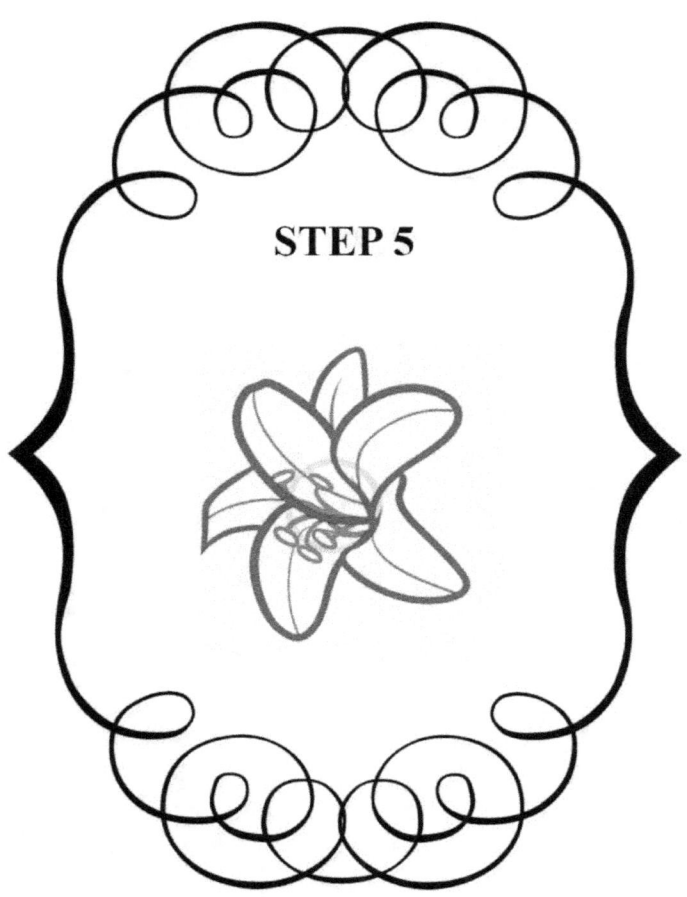

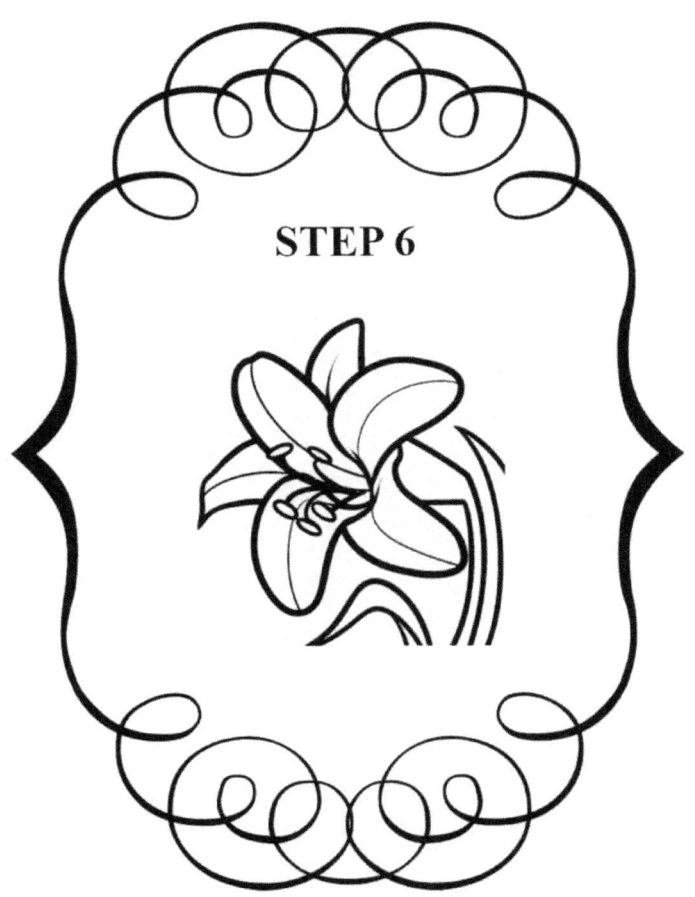

STEP 6

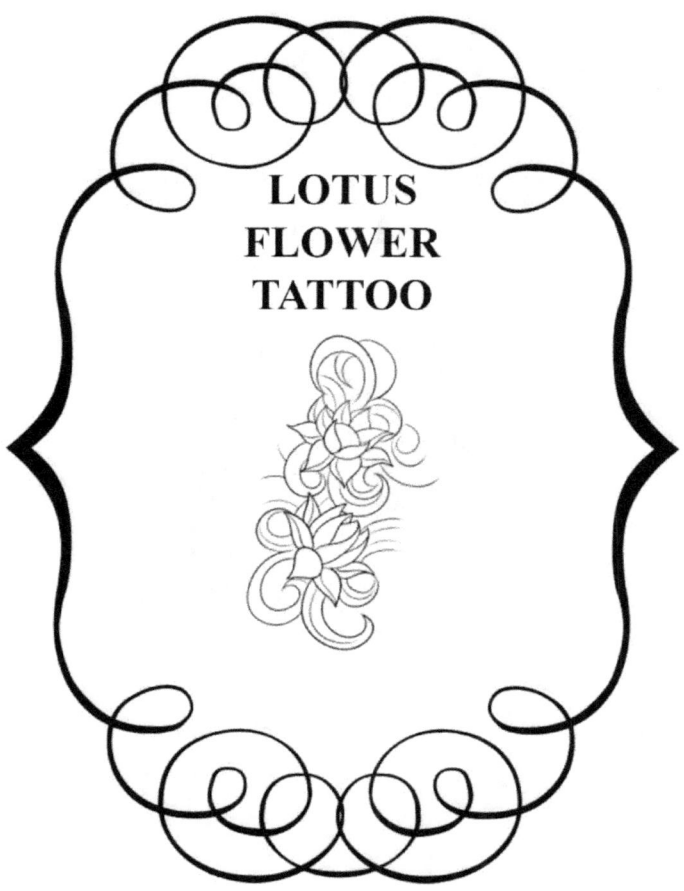

LOTUS FLOWER TATTOO

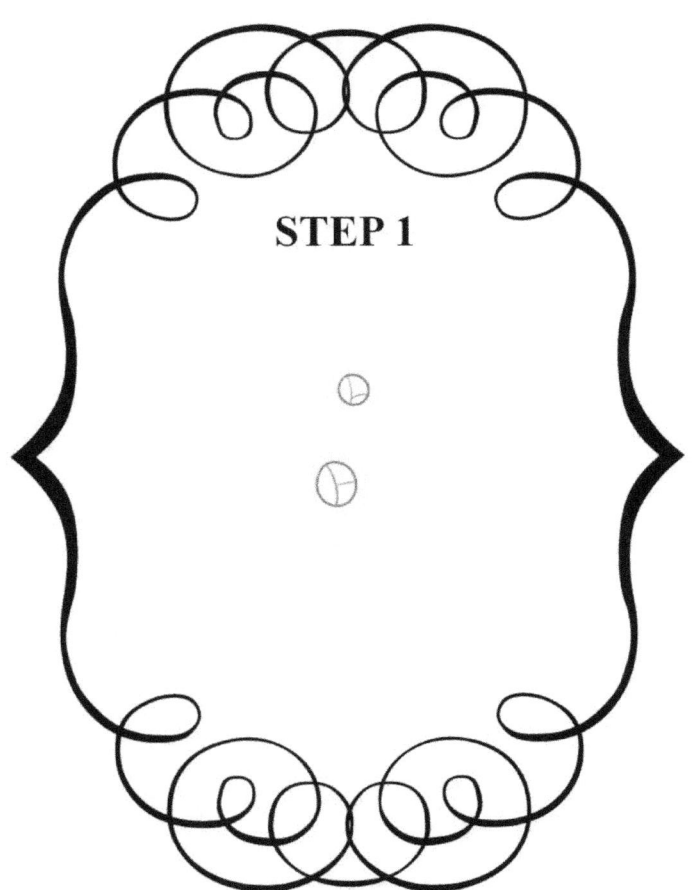

STEP 1

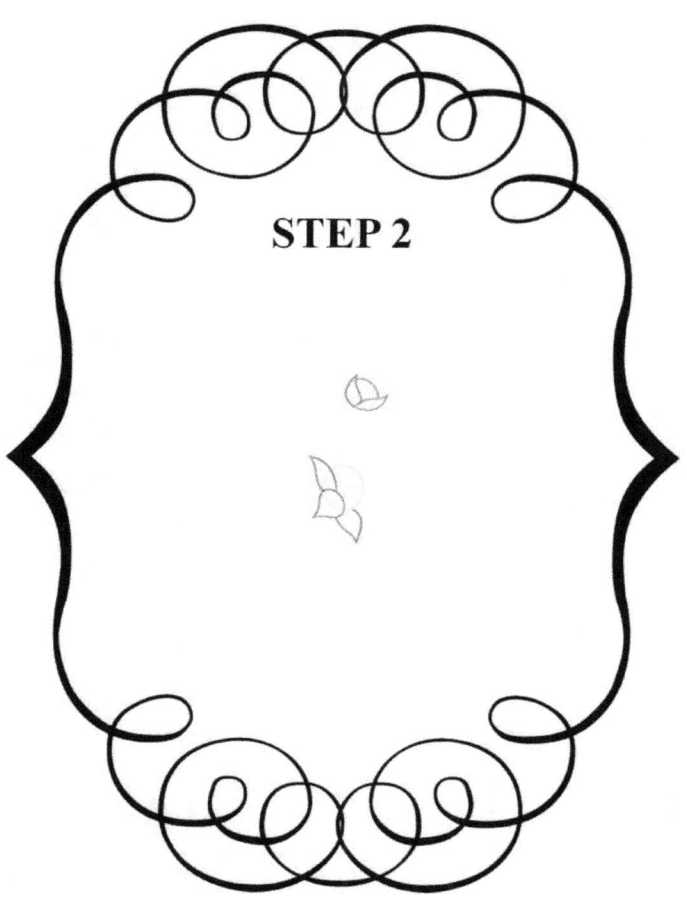

STEP 2

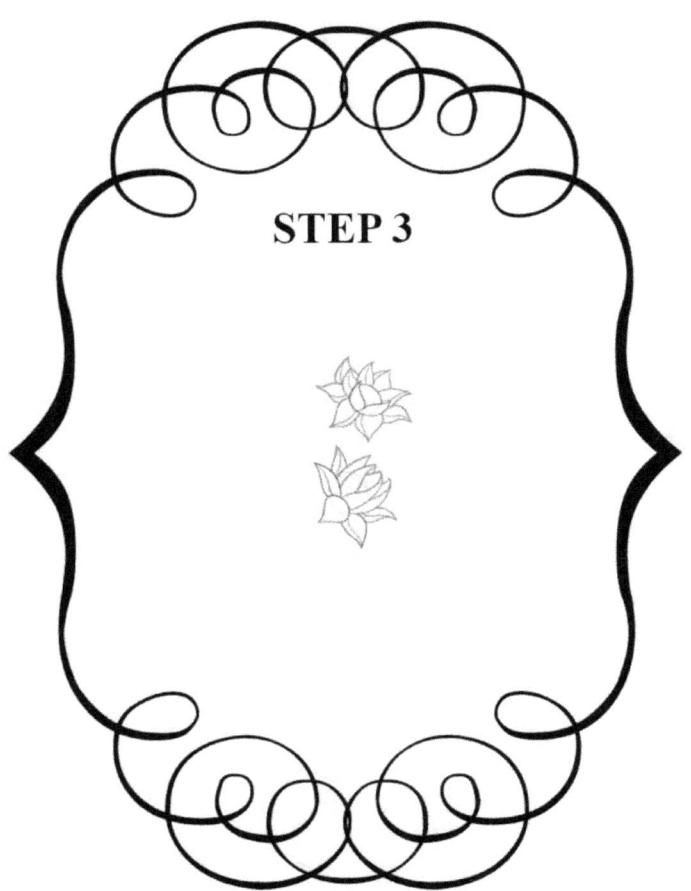

STEP 3

STEP 4

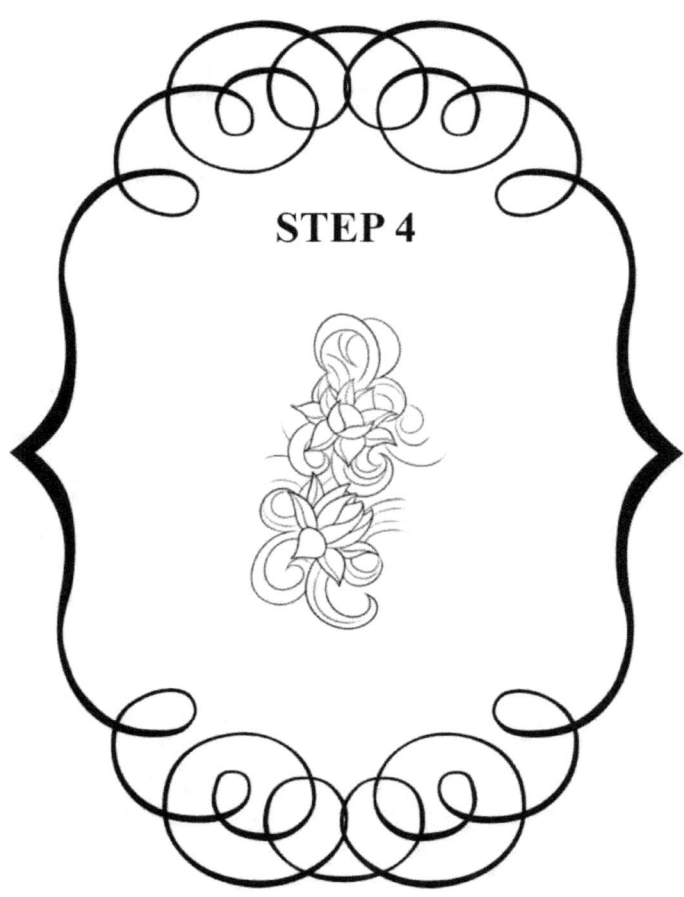

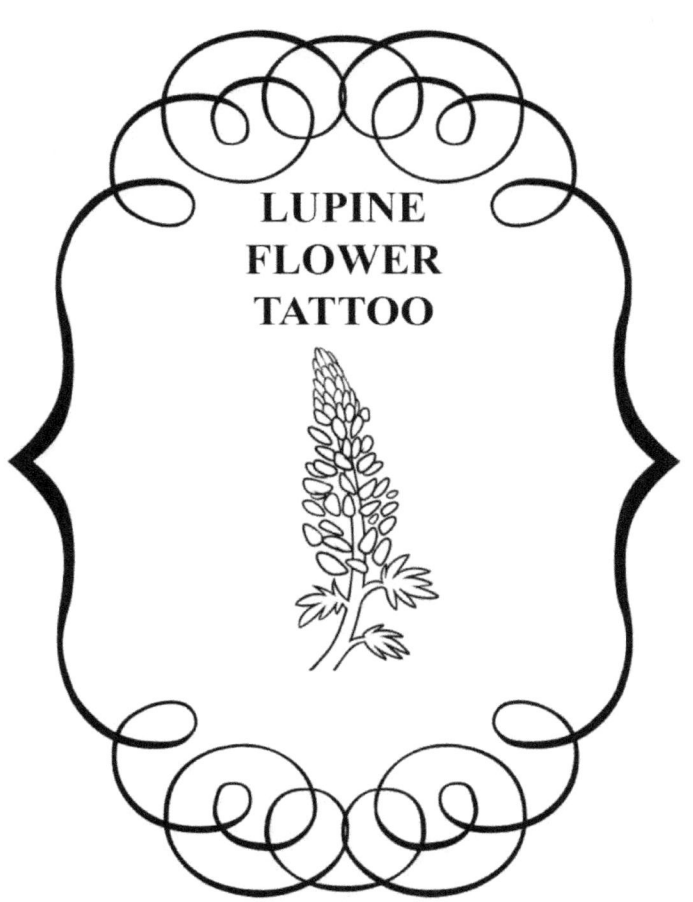

LUPINE
FLOWER
TATTOO

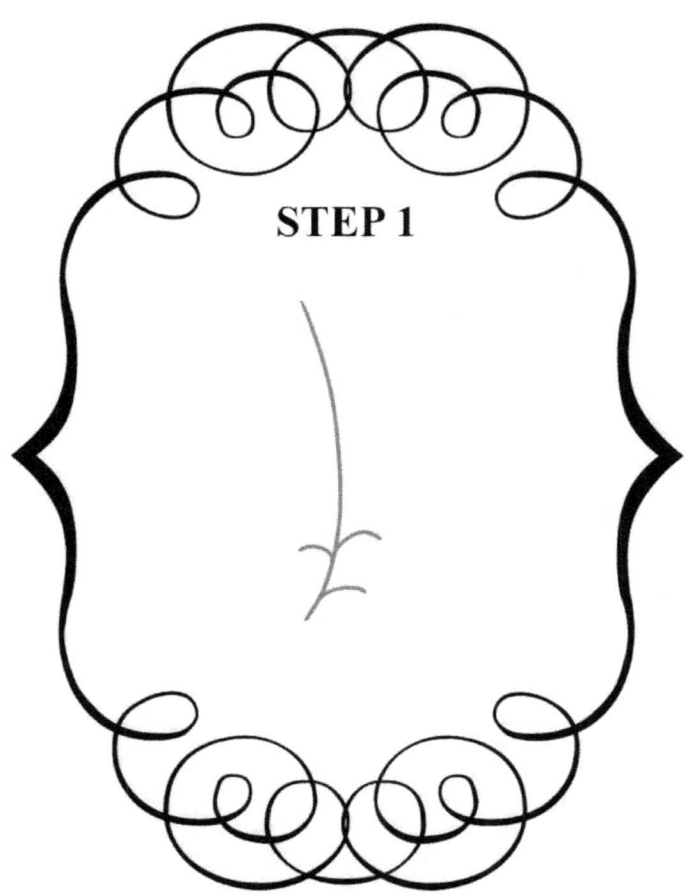

STEP 1

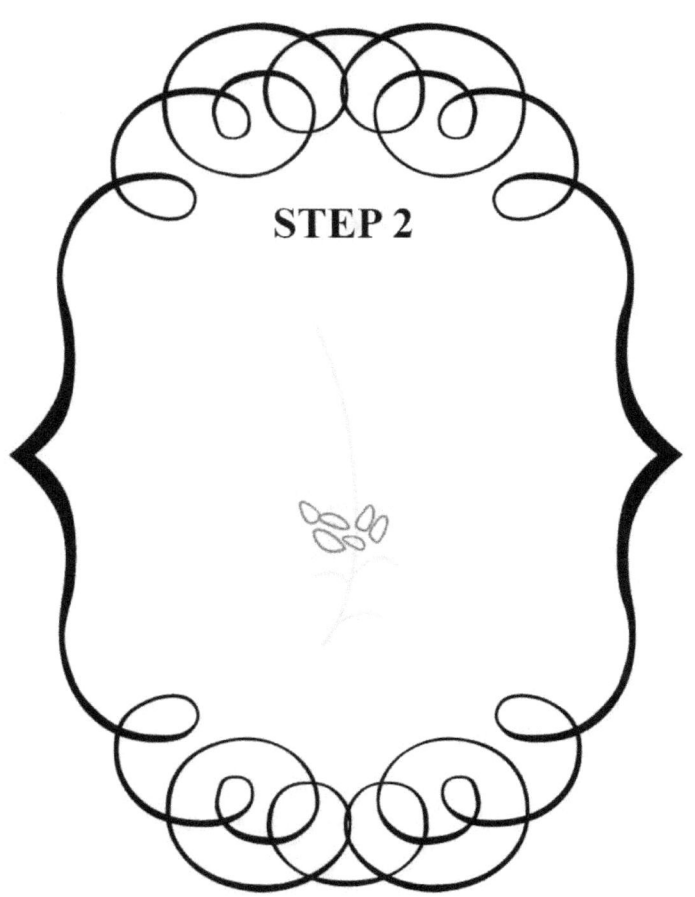

STEP 2

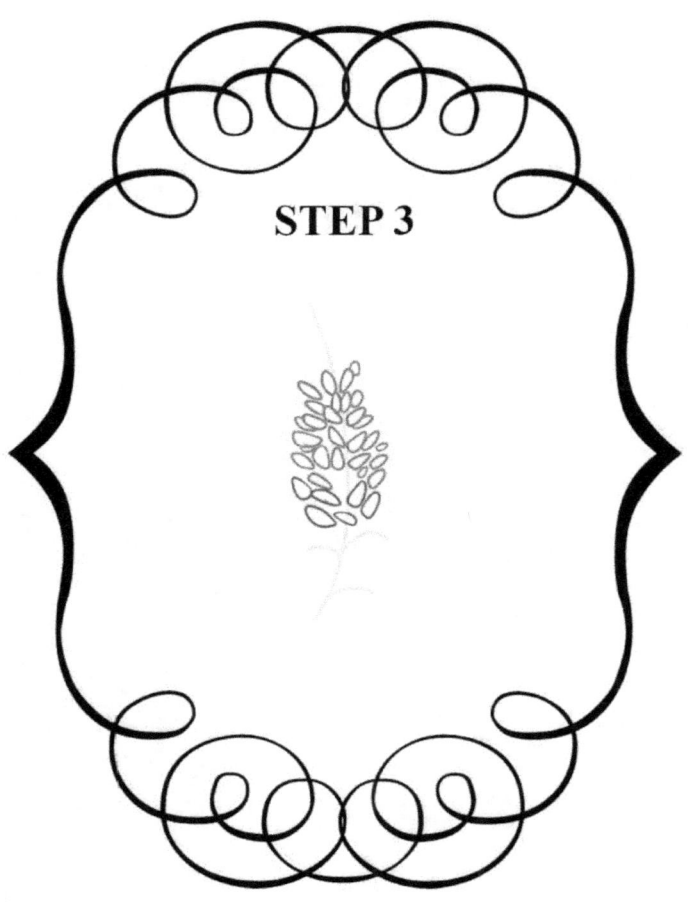

STEP 3

STEP 4

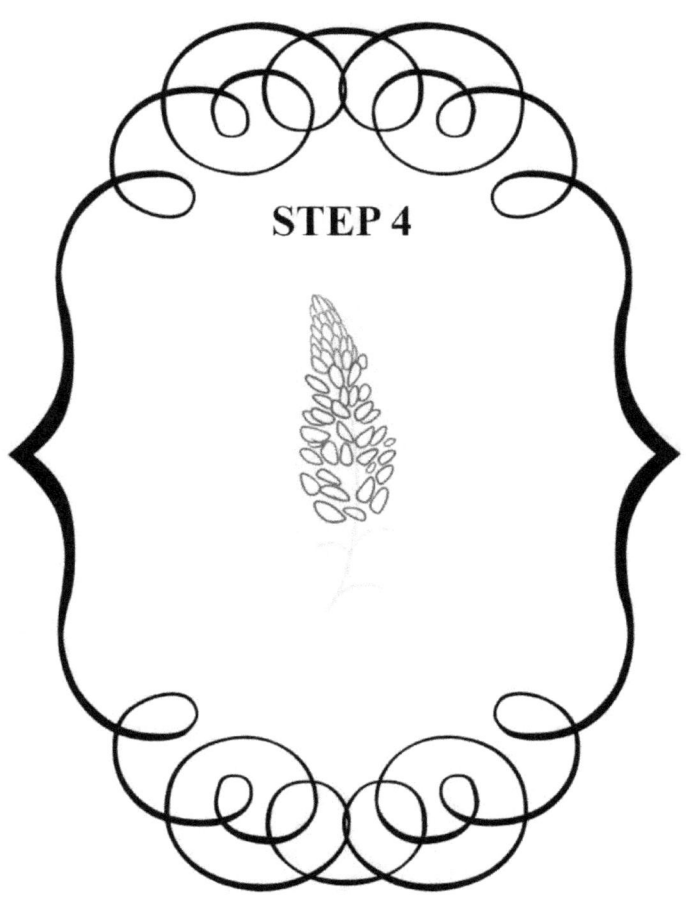

STEP 5

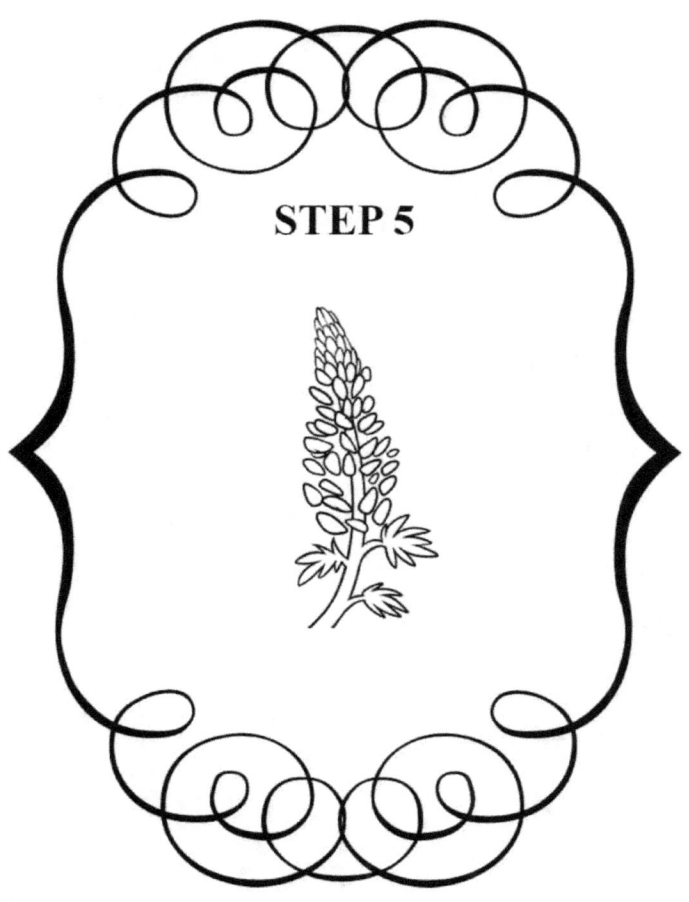

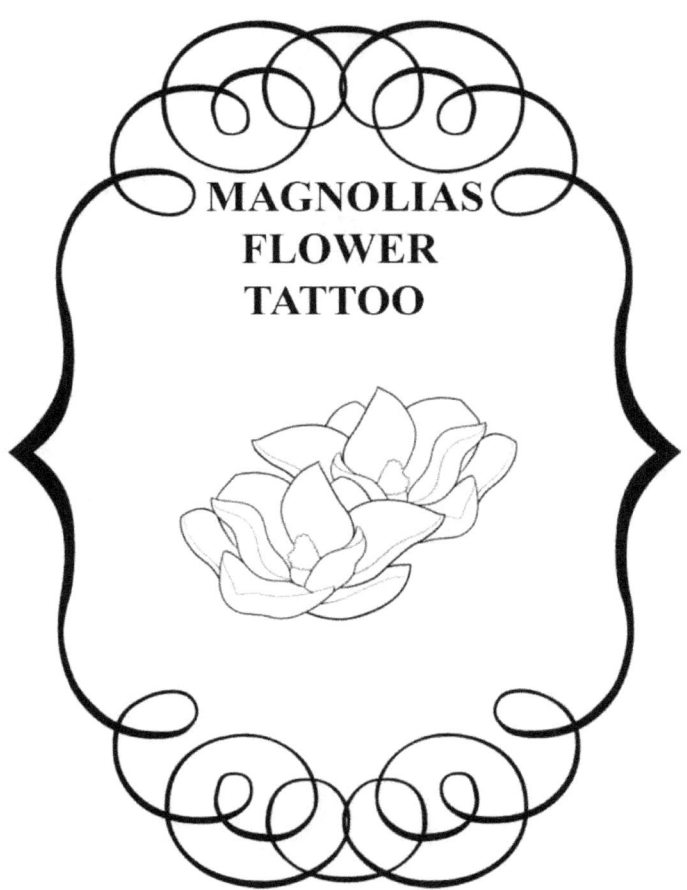

MAGNOLIAS FLOWER TATTOO

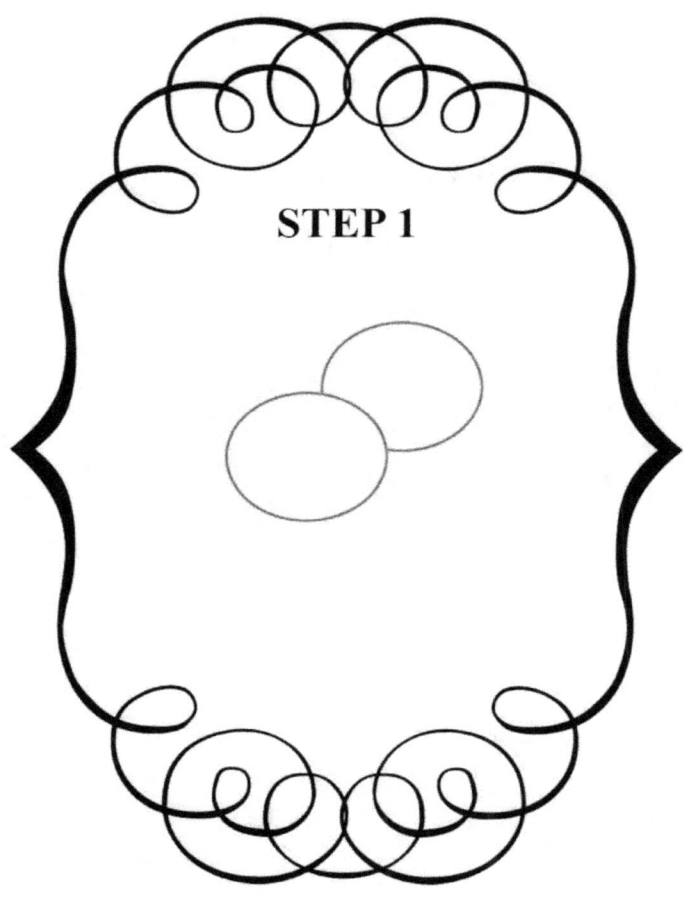

STEP 1

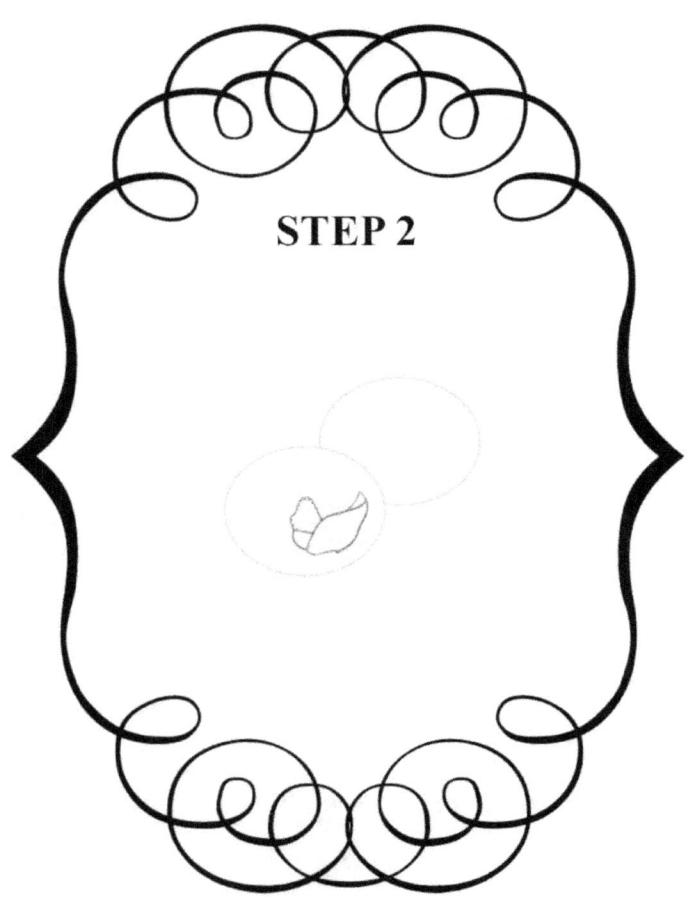

STEP 2

STEP 3

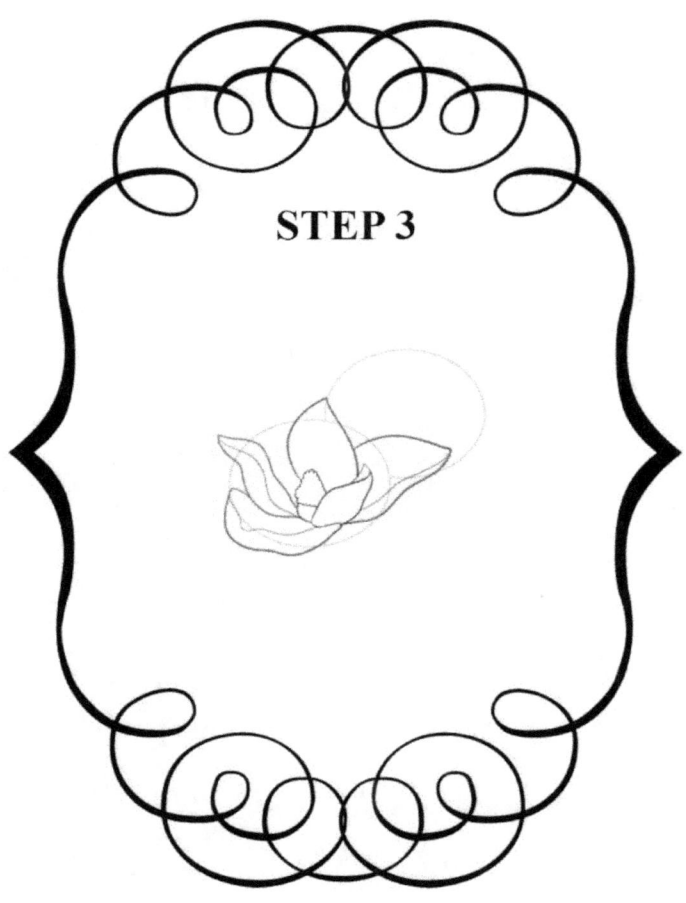

STEP 4

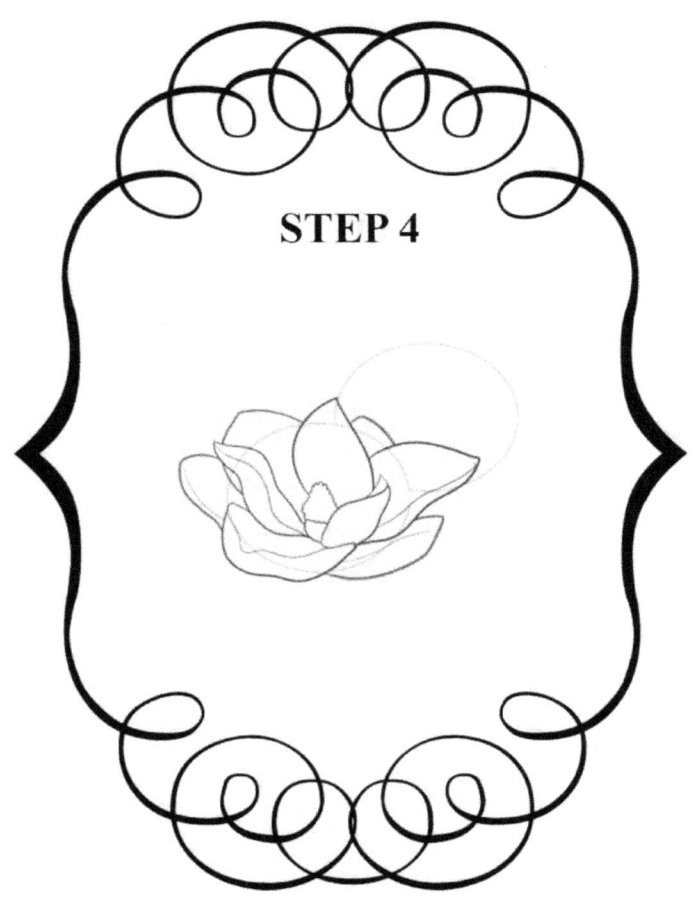

STEP 5

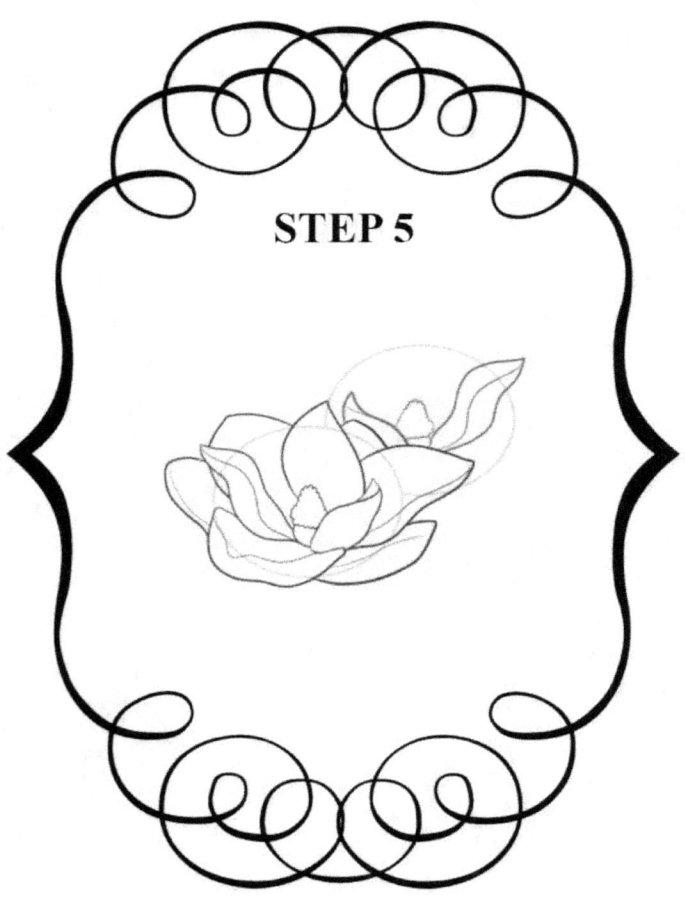

STEP 6

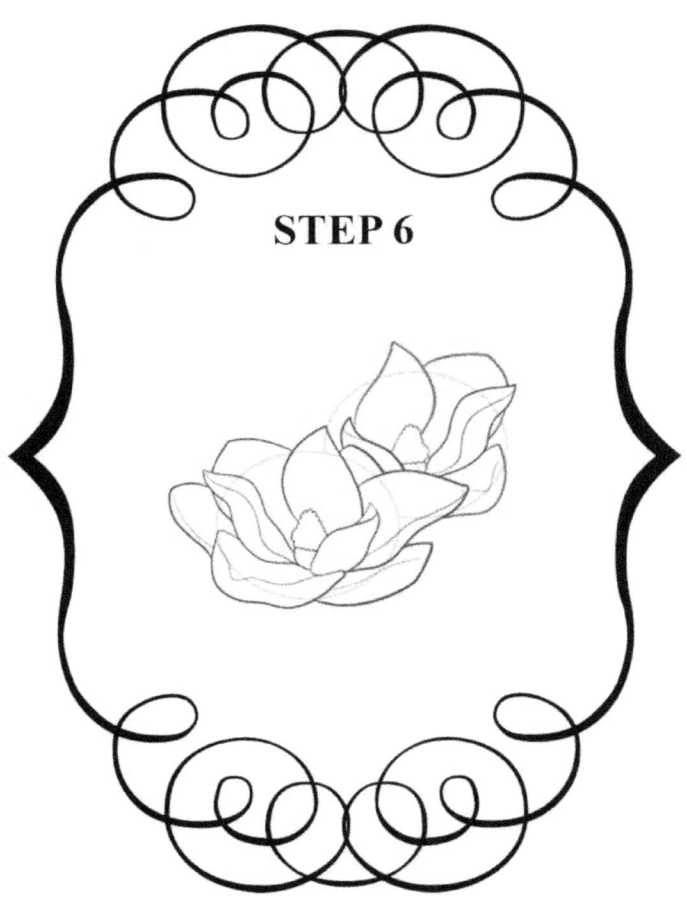

STEP 7

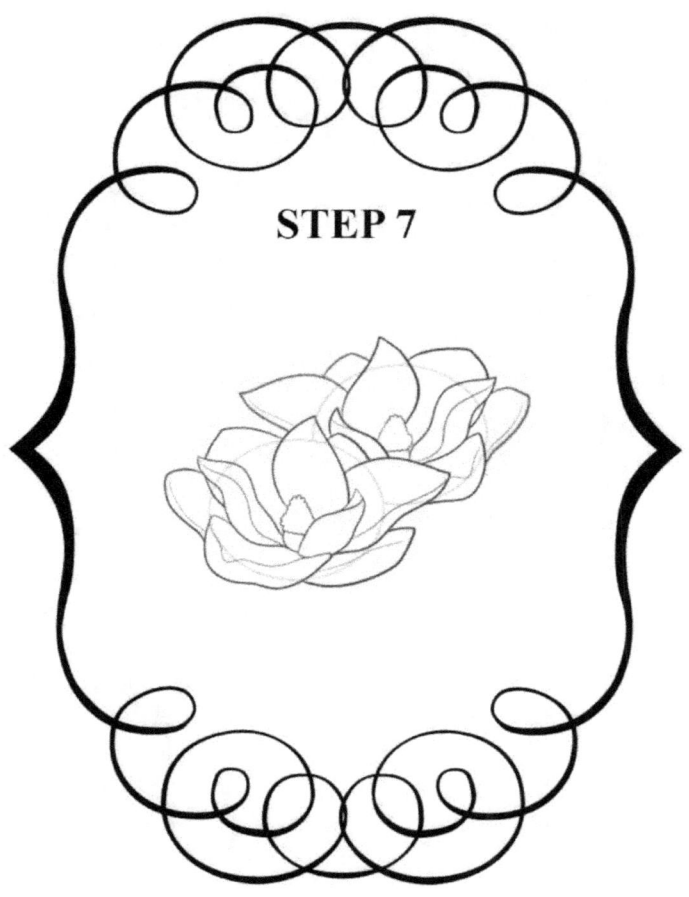

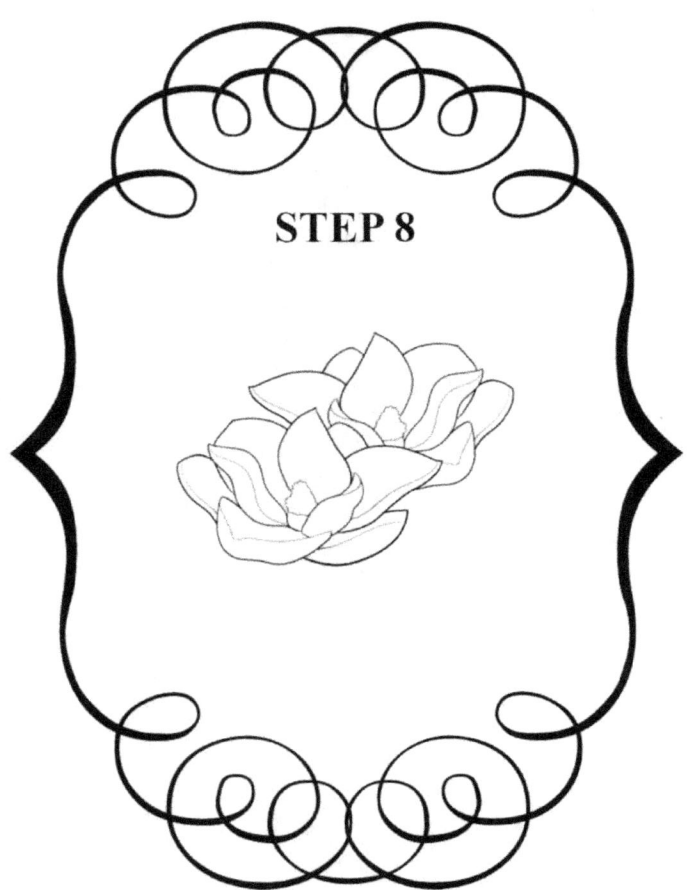

STEP 8

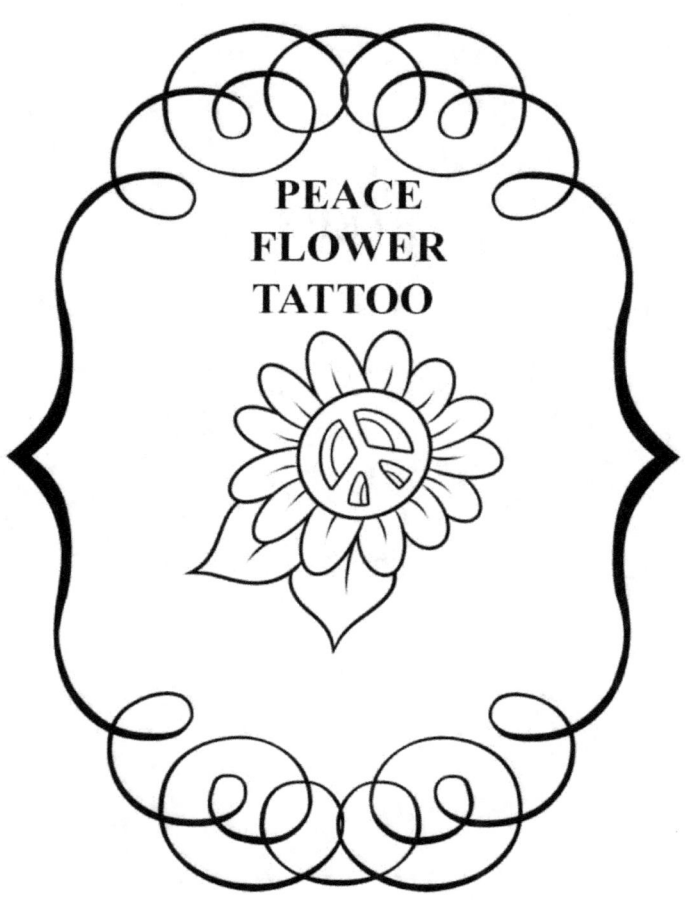

PEACE
FLOWER
TATTOO

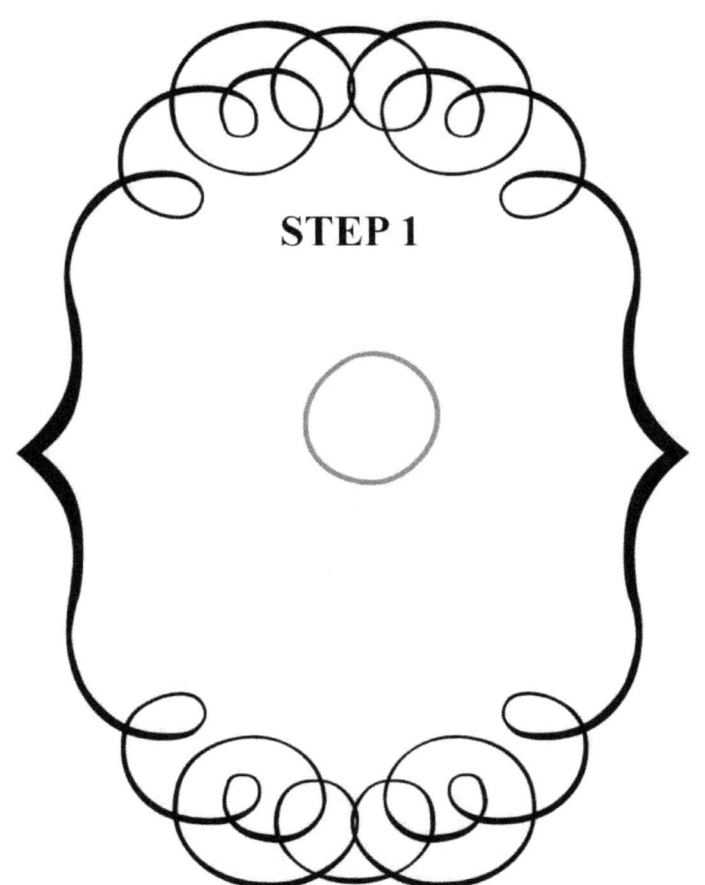

STEP 1

74

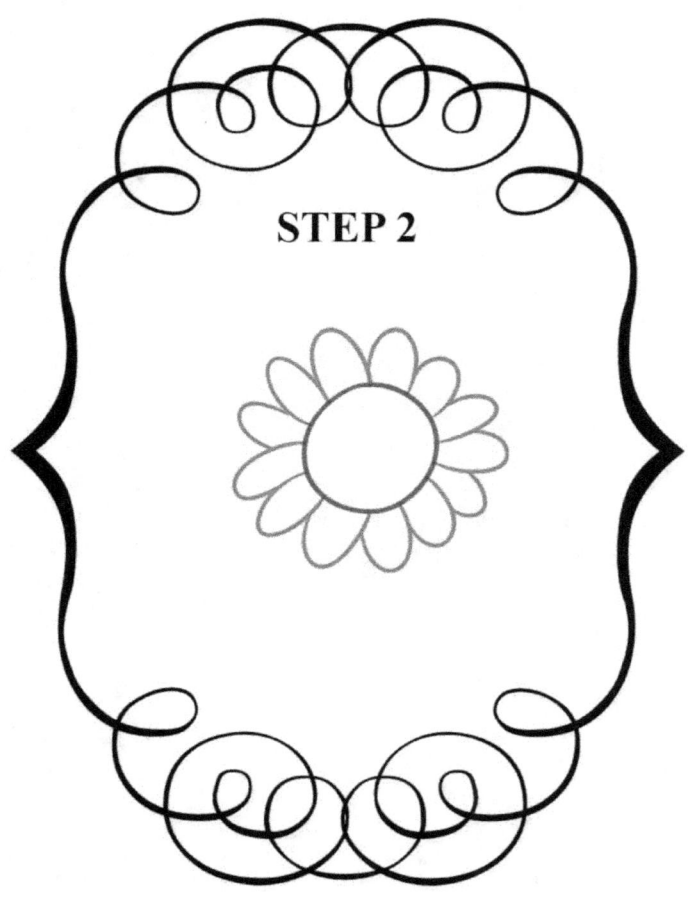

STEP 2

STEP 3

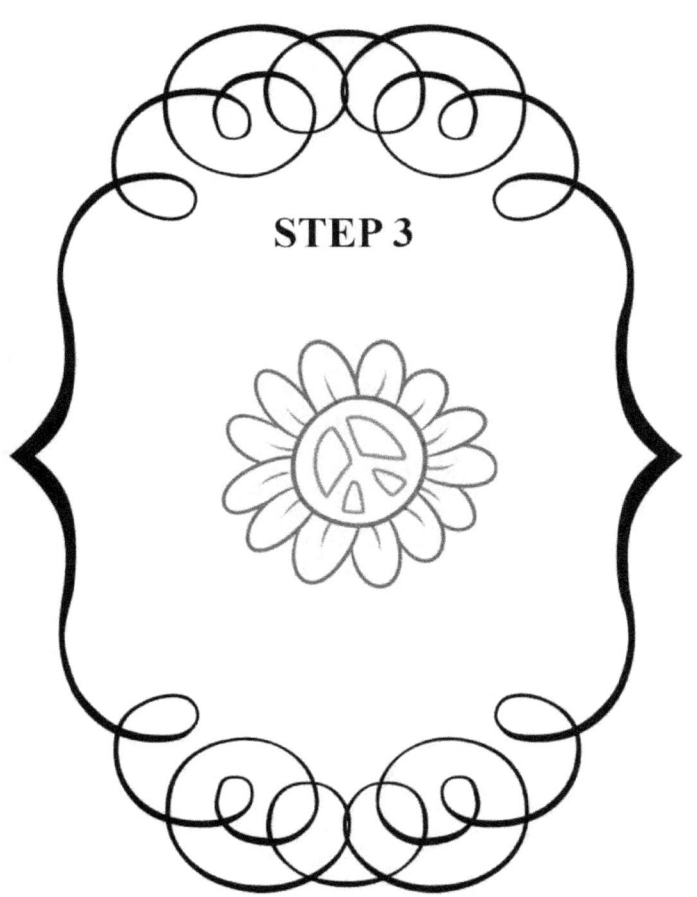

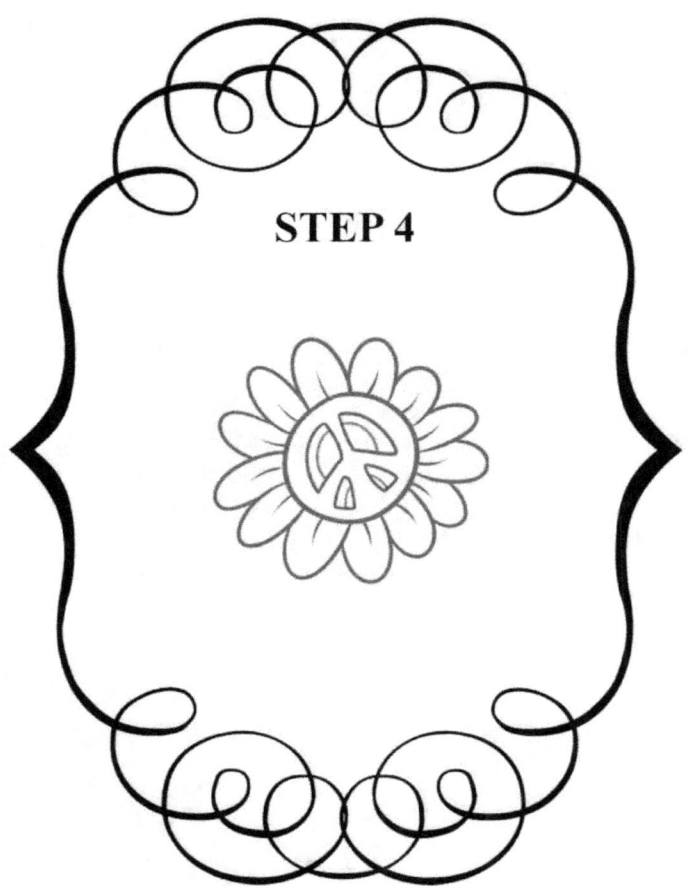

STEP 4

STEP 5

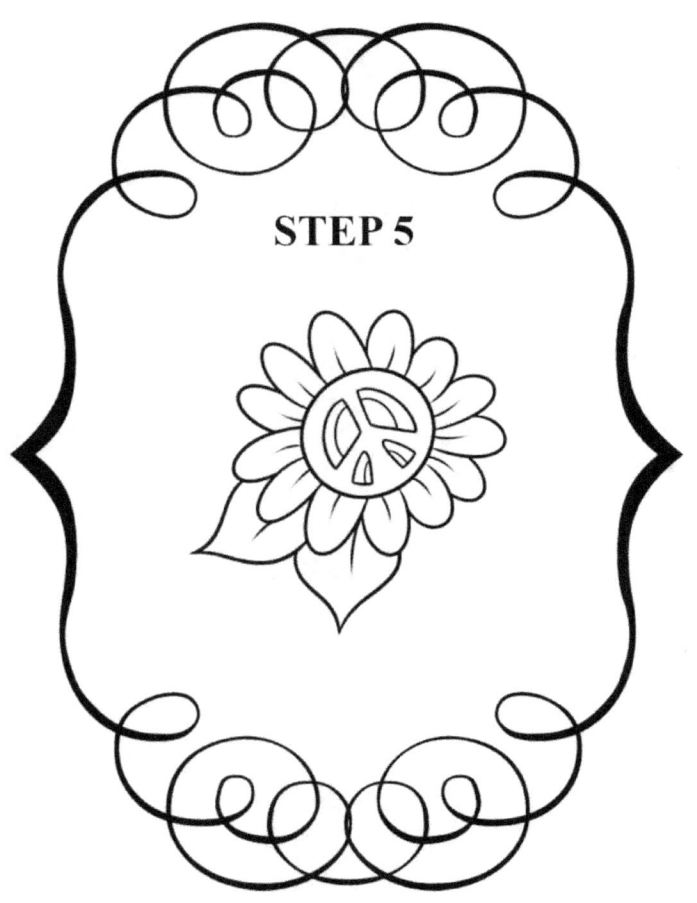

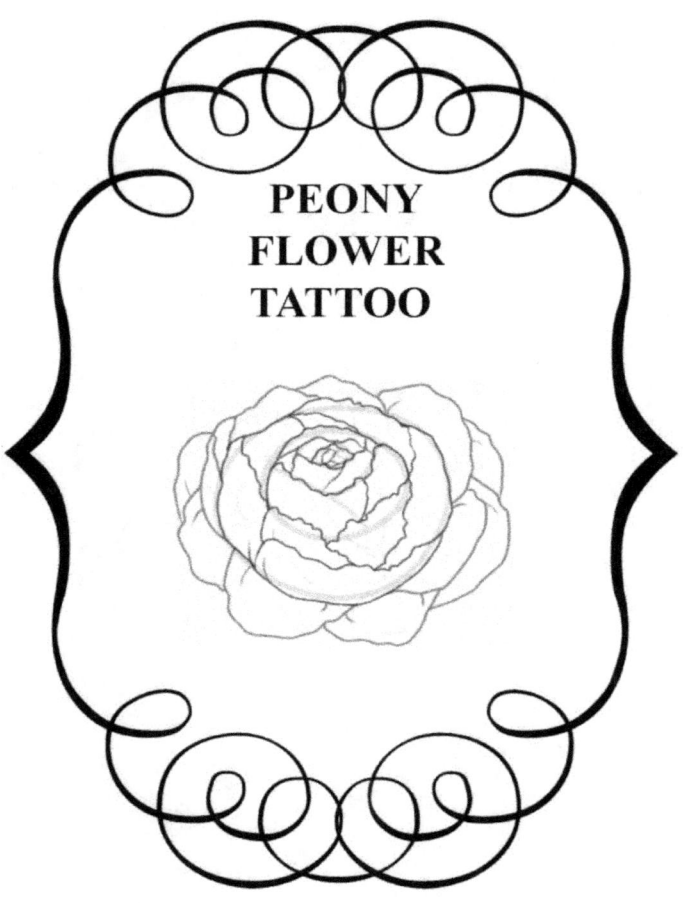

PEONY
FLOWER
TATTOO

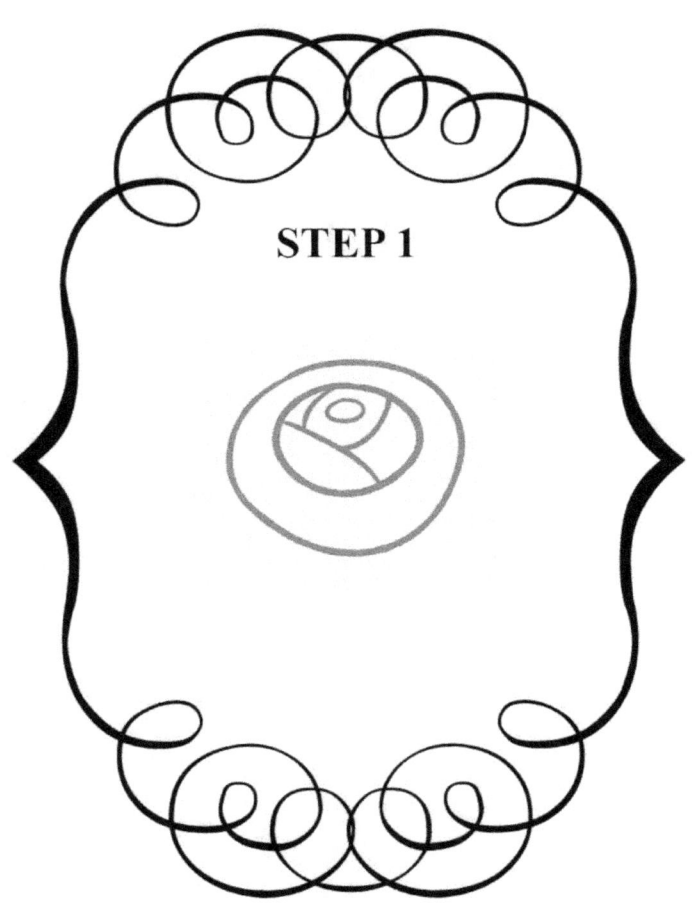

STEP 1

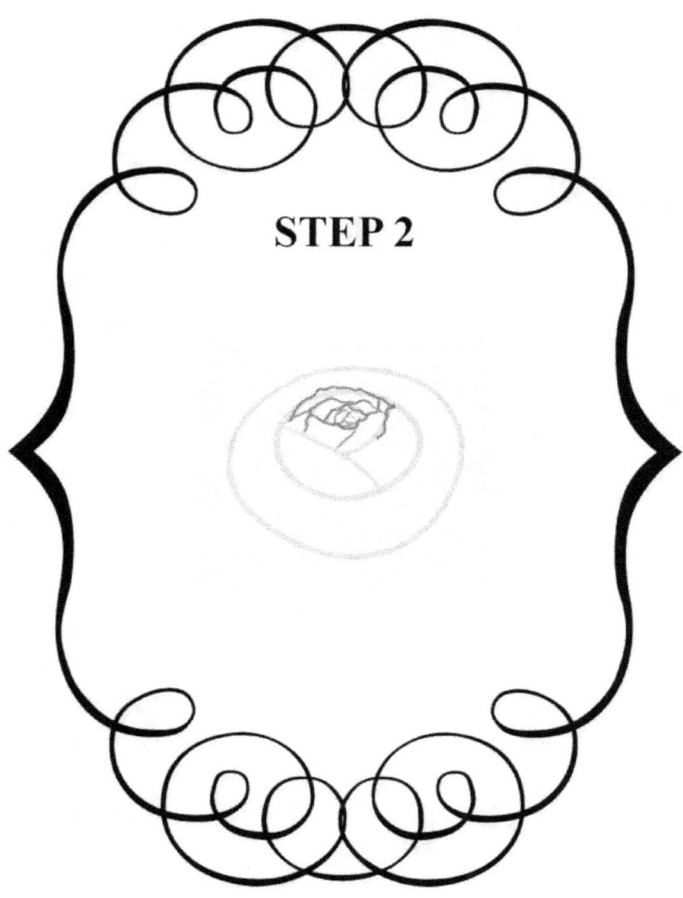

STEP 2

STEP 3

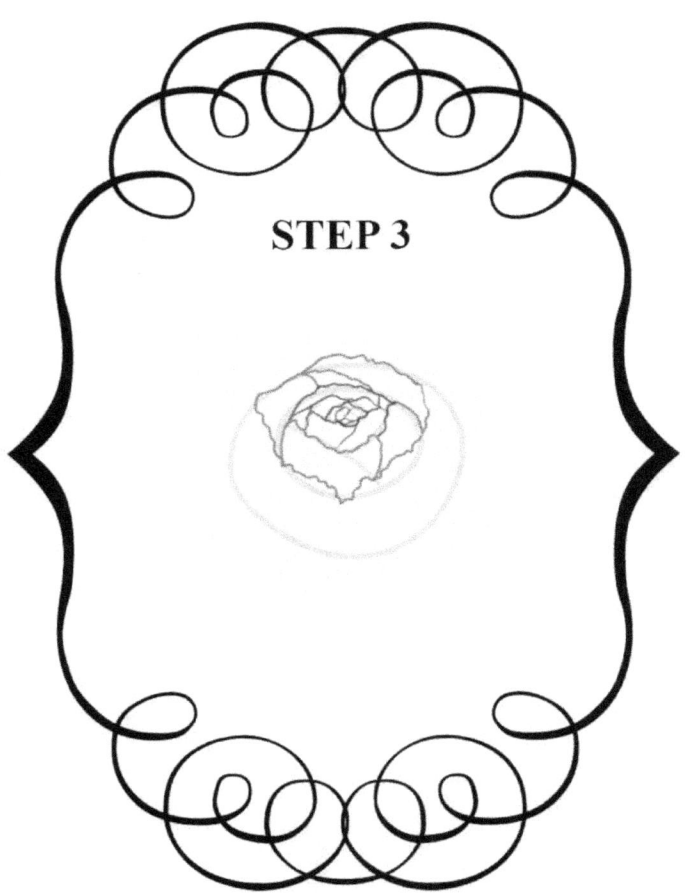

STEP 4

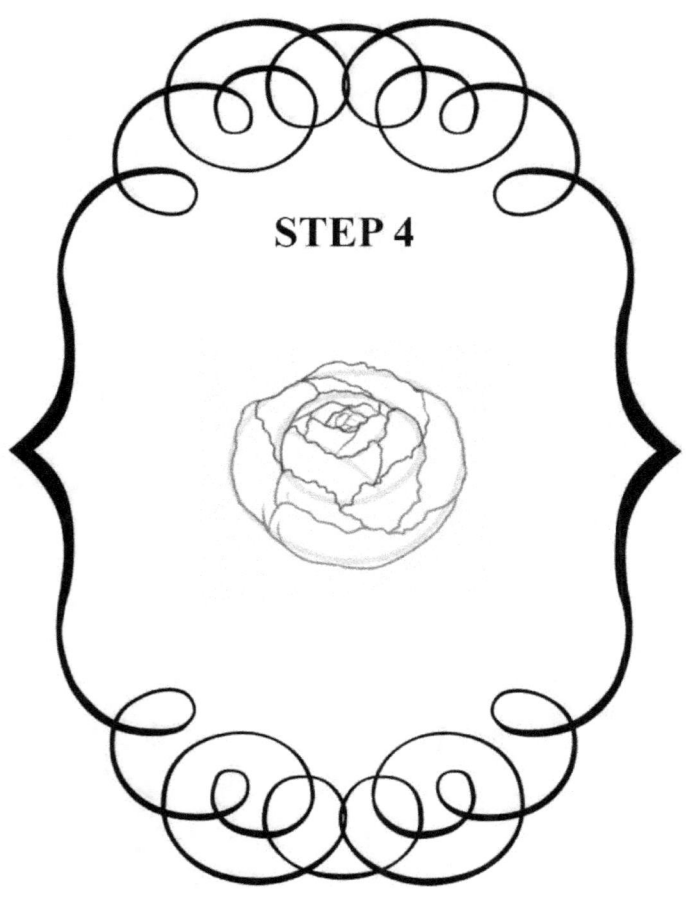

STEP 5

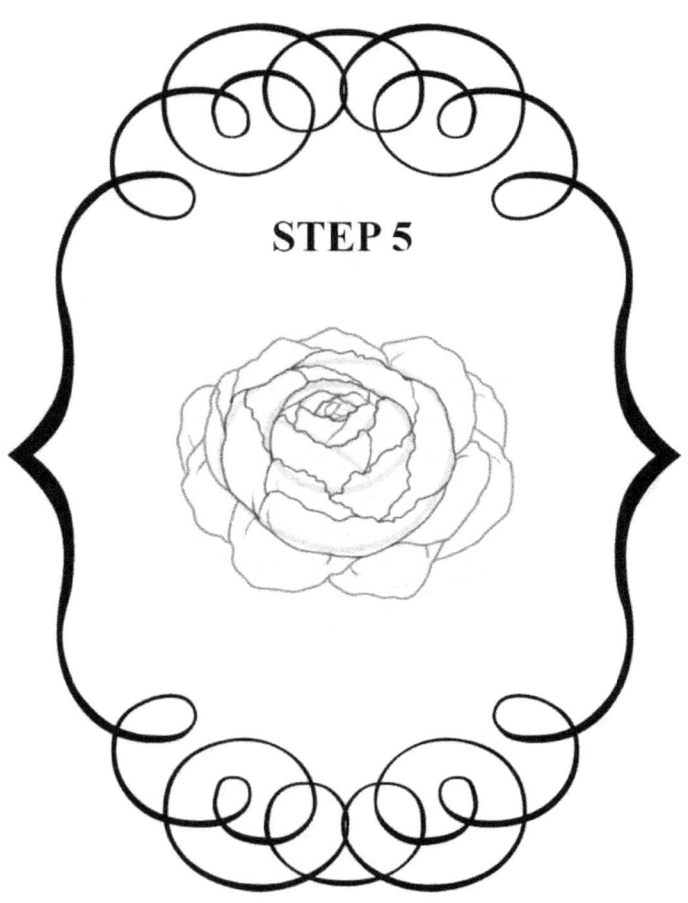

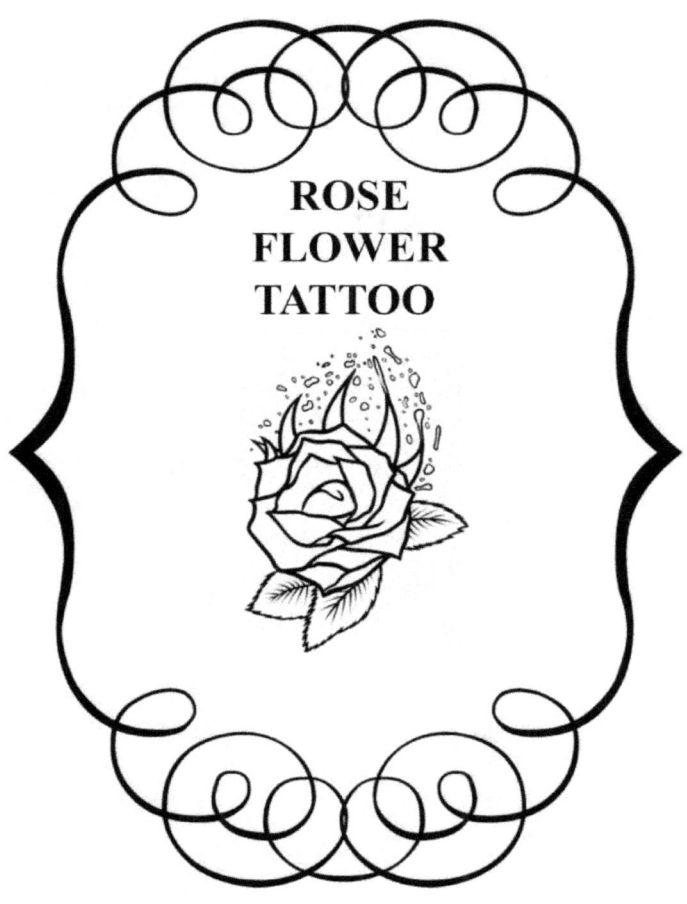

ROSE
FLOWER
TATTOO

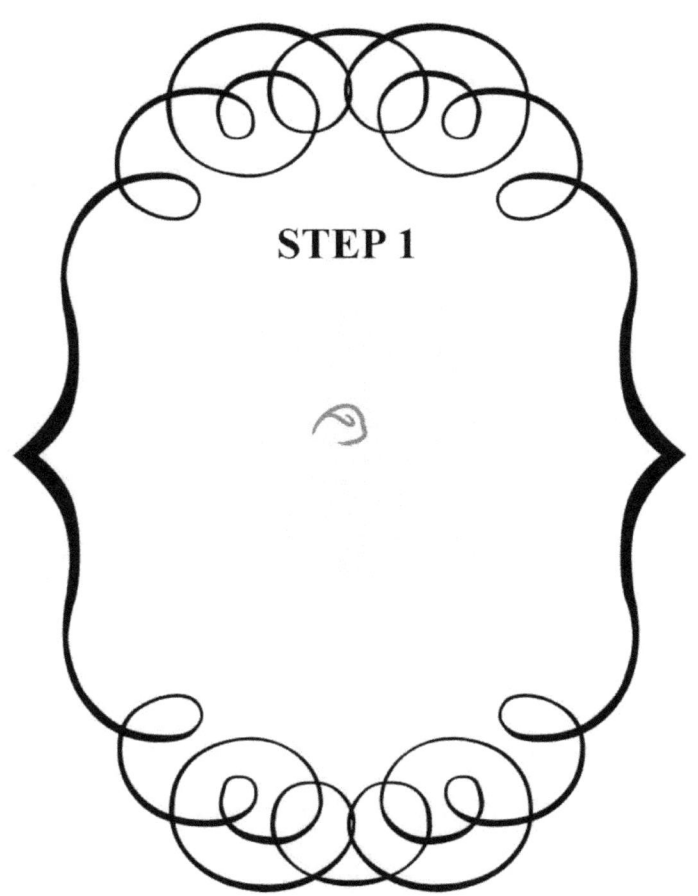

STEP 1

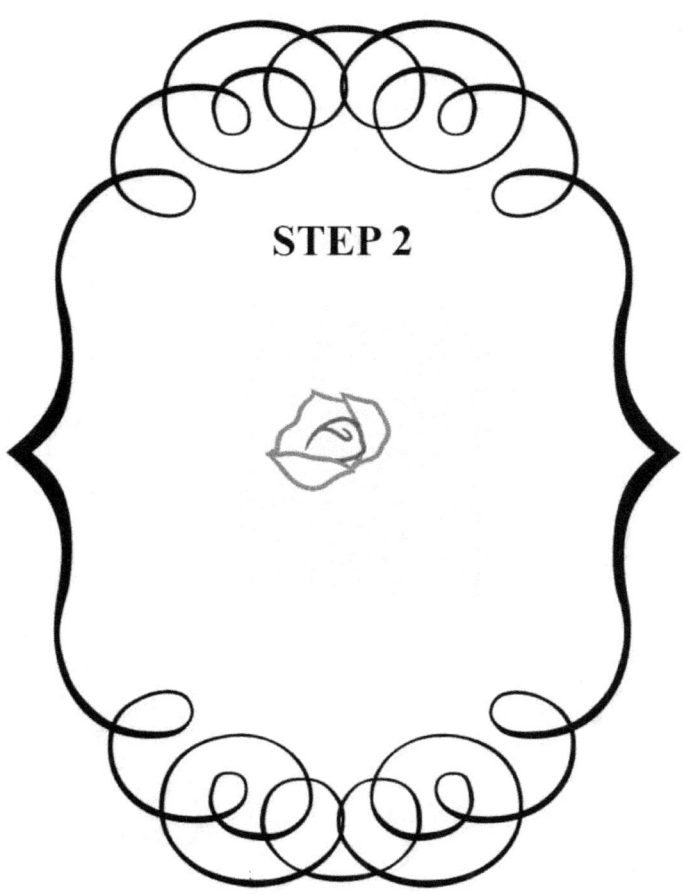

STEP 2

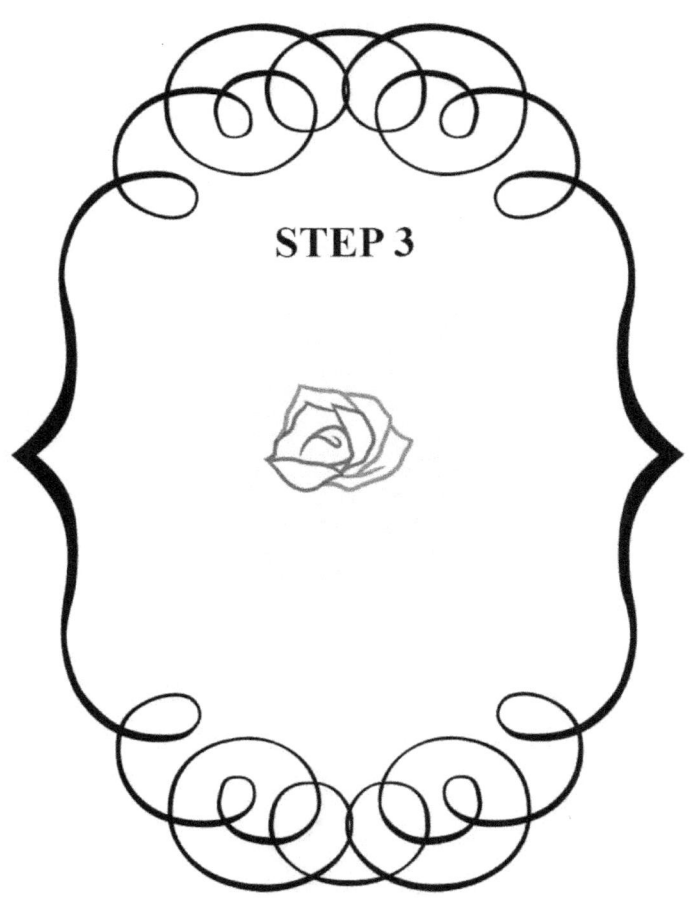

STEP 3

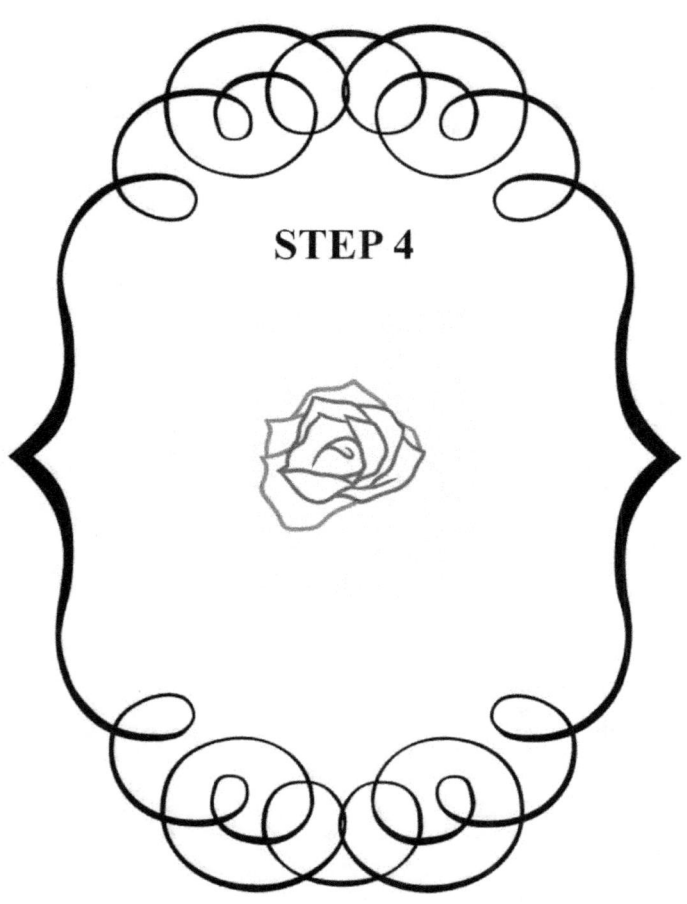

STEP 4

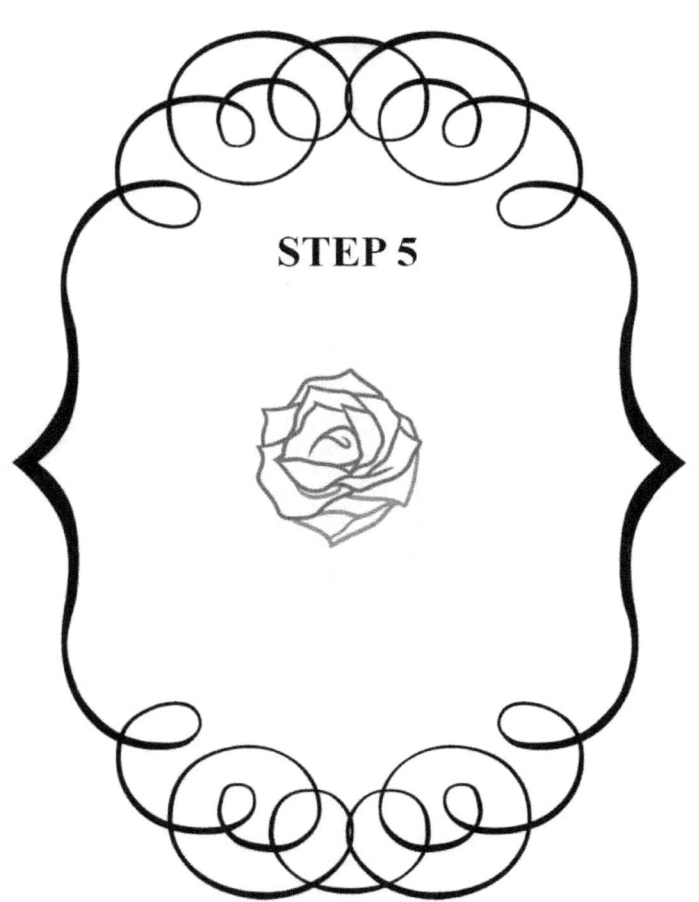

STEP 5

STEP 6

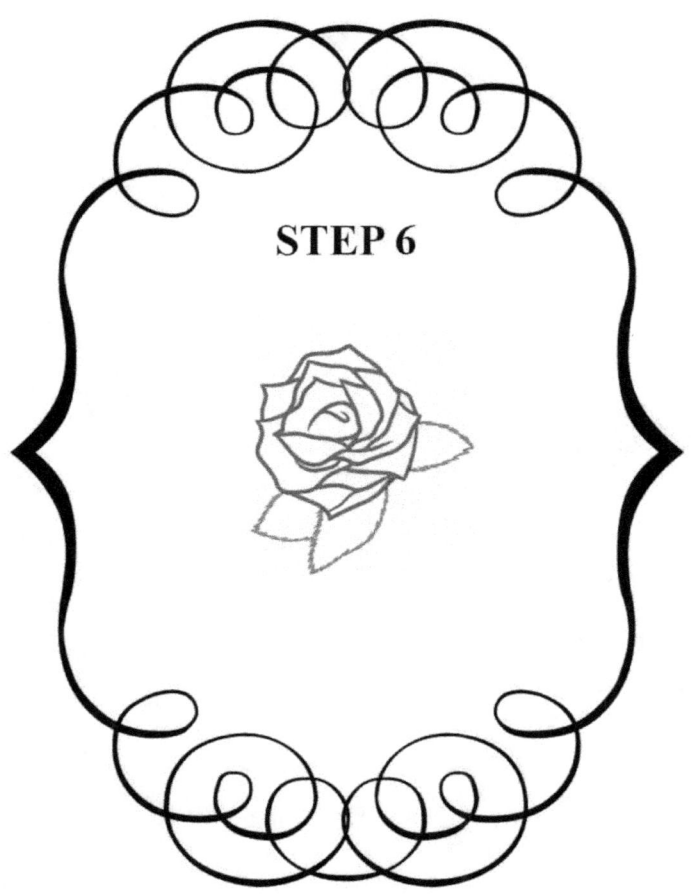

STEP 7

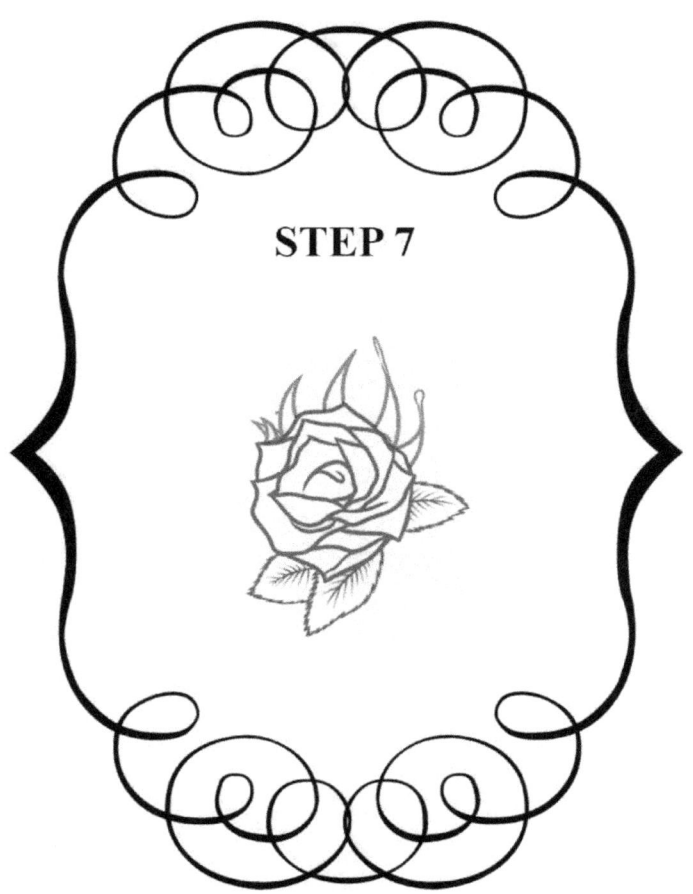

STEP 8

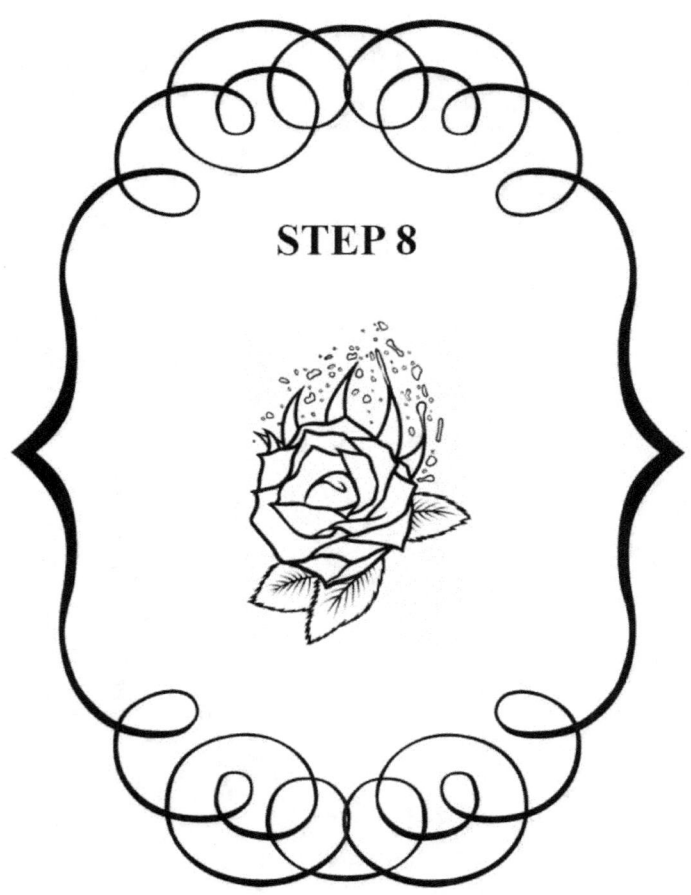

SUNFLOWER
TATTOO

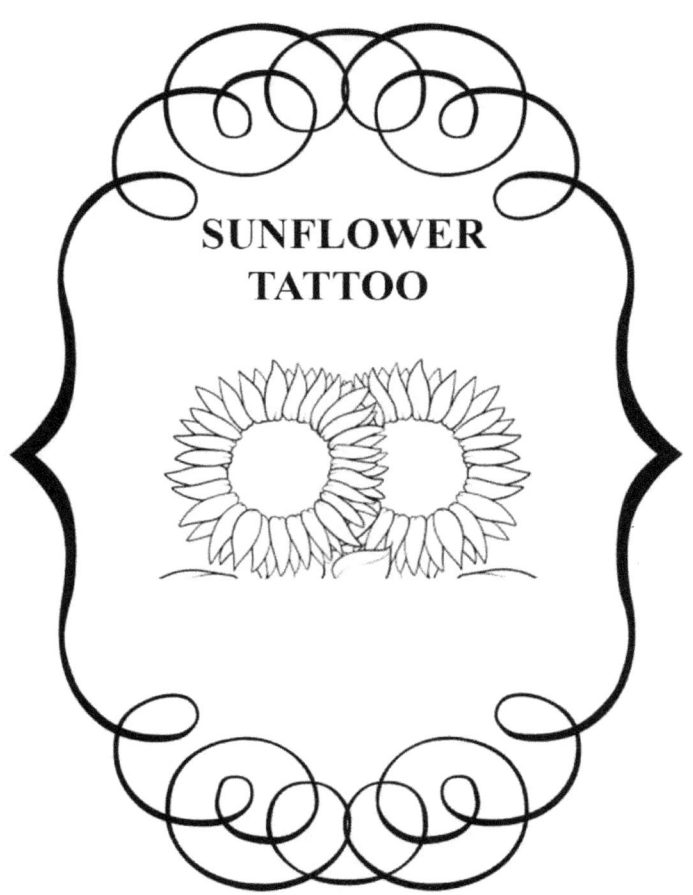

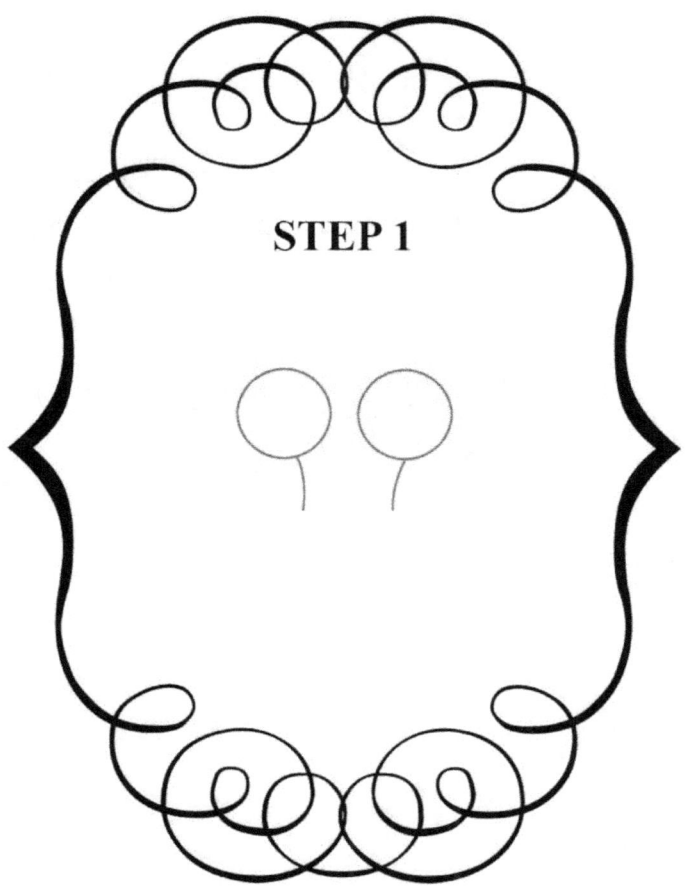

STEP 1

STEP 2

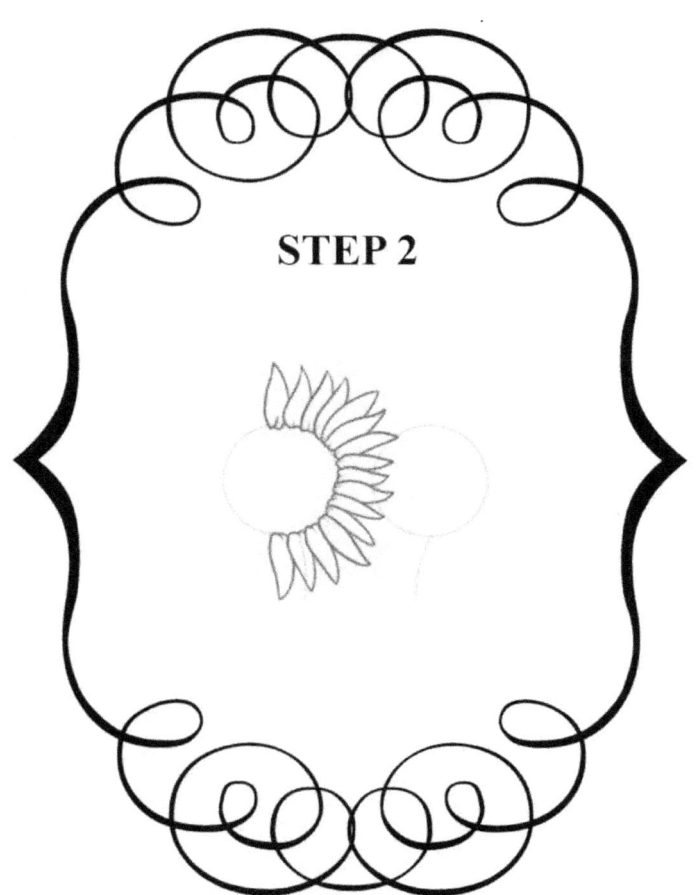

STEP 3

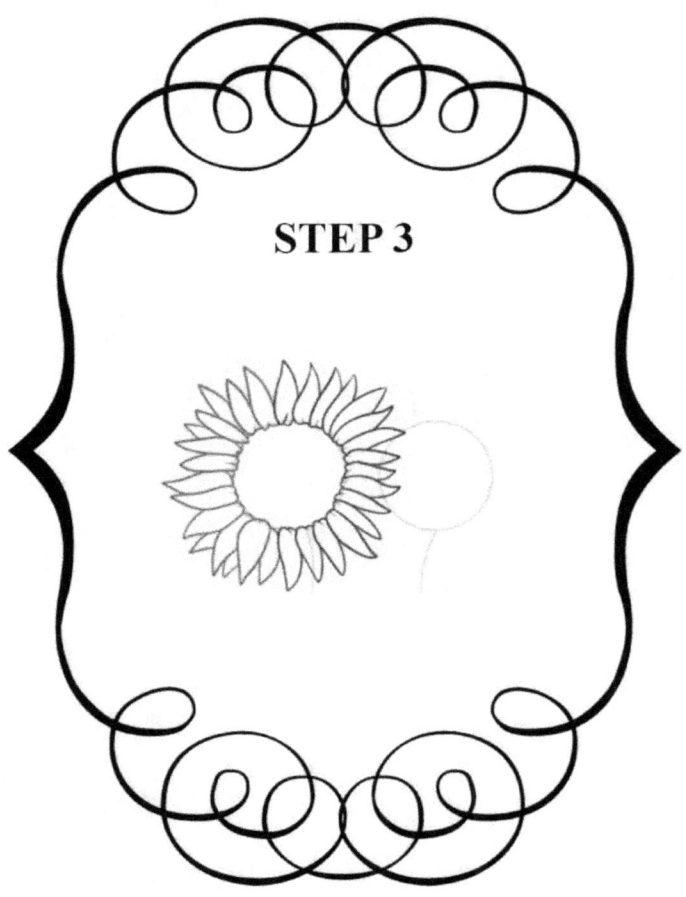

STEP 4

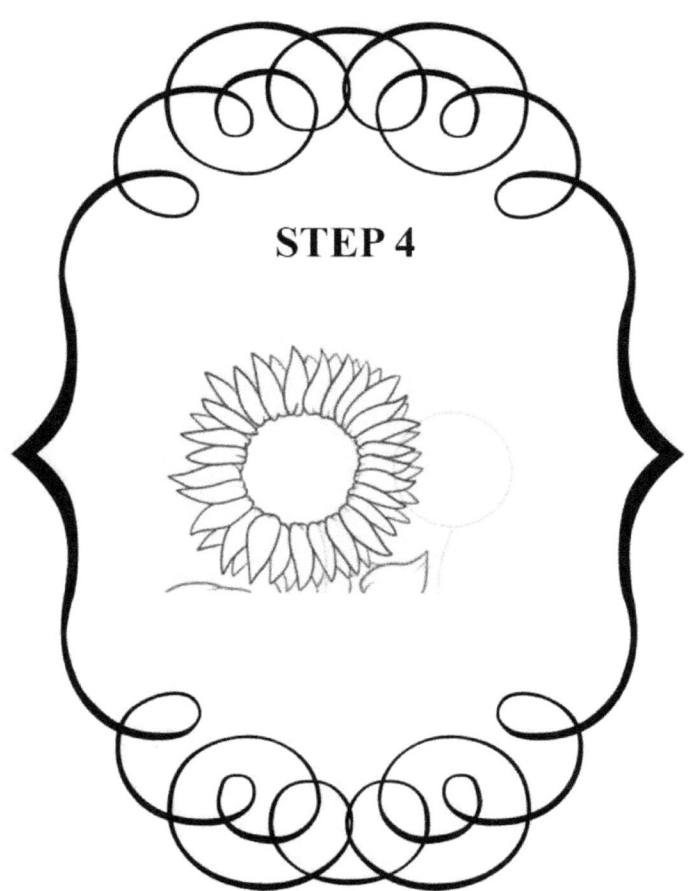

STEP 5

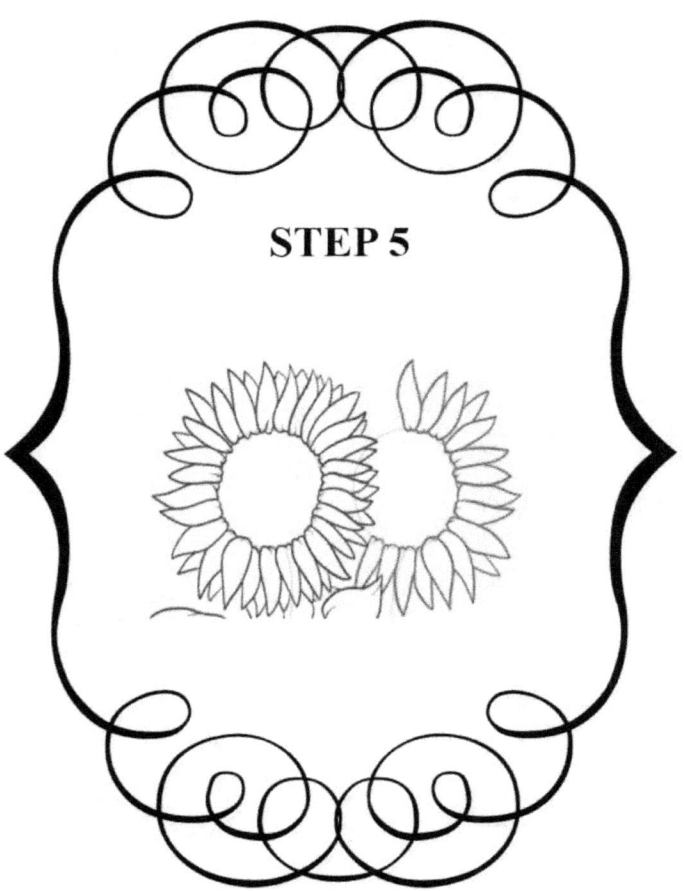

STEP 6

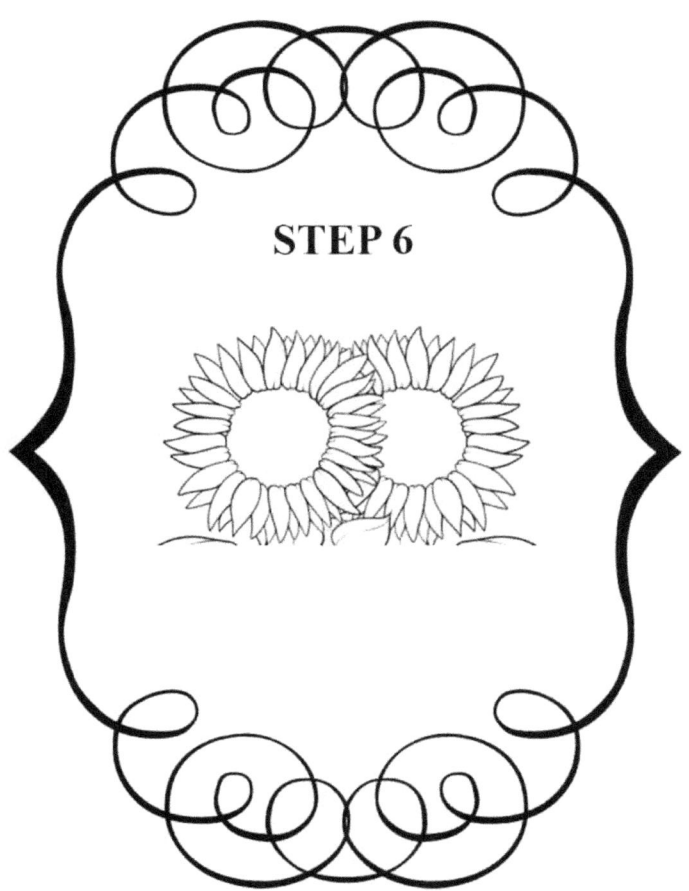